T0095003

SERVING WITH

Honor

UNDER A CLOAK OF SILENCE

Dr. Lorenzo L. McFarland with
Brian E. Markowski, T. David Gilmer, and
Kenneth N. Brooks

authorHOUSE®

AuthorHouse™
1663 Liberty Drive
Bloomington, IN 47403
www.authorhouse.com
Phone: 1-800-839-8640

First published by AuthorHouse   11/22/2011

ISBN: 978-1-4685-0757-7 (sc)
ISBN: 978-1-4685-0756-0 (hc)
ISBN: 978-1-4685-0755-3 (ebk)

Library of Congress Control Number: 2011961509

Printed in the United States of America

Acknowledgments

I thank God for my amazing life. It is not one that I would have picked out for myself, but I am grateful all the same. God does not place on you more than you can bear. I am stronger because of my experiences!

I stand on the shoulders of my family—Lorenzo (Dad), Odell (mom), Jewel, Betty, Dennis, and Lindsay. Even when I felt misunderstood, I felt loved. Dad, when I told you I was gay, you said, "You are my son, and I love you." I will never forget that day!

A special thanks to my cousin (son), Ja'Marcus Roberson. He reminds me of myself at his age. He has overcome so much in his short life. I am a better person because of him.

For accepting and believing in me and for always expecting more, I appreciate my military family: Cheryl McCrary, Gary Matsamura, Richard Van Dyke, Shelia Grady, Claudio and Rebecca Castillo, Michael and Felicia Landez, Lorena Bailey, DeeDee Millican (mom), and Jacqueline Jackson. Special thanks to Robert Spencer, my brother from another mother.

I would like to thank Dr. John Parkhurst for lending his unique talents and insight to this book. Also, a big thank you to Gayle Lyke

for helping with edits through-out the entire
project.

Finally, special thanks to Brian "Ski"
Markowski, David Gilmer, and Kenneth Brooks
for agreeing to be a part of this book. When
I first approached them about the project,
there was general excitement, but shock soon
set in once they realized they would have
to share much of what they had kept secret
their entire military career. They survived,
however, and the book would be nothing without
their input.

Preface

In 1993, Congress enacted into law Don't Ask, Don't Tell (DADT), which excluded gays, lesbians, and bisexuals from military service if they disclosed their sexuality or engaged in homosexual acts. The thought behind the law was that the presence of openly homosexual personnel would create an unacceptable risk to the armed forces' high standards of morale, good order, discipline, and unit cohesion. With the passage of DADT, there was a sense that the active witch hunts had stopped; still, over the next sixteen years, more than sixteen thousand gays and lesbians were kicked out of the military. At the same time, sixteen years of DADT put to rest the notion that gays in the military lowered the standards of morale, good order, and discipline. The rank and file knew we gays were among them, and they knew we were great military personnel; we did our jobs well and in all branches of service.

Fast-forward to 2011 and the fight to end DADT, you saw a new tactic to keep the policy in place. The focus was limited to a single argument: allowing gays to serve openly would be a deterrent to unit cohesion. The debate was divided along several parties, gays and their supporters, conservatives, and religious

organizations. Defenders of DADT went before
Congress to describe what they considered to
be the erosion of unit cohesion.

This book is written as a contrast to that
testimony. It depicts my life as a gay military
Veteran, Along with three of my friends, all
serving with honor and in silence. You will see
that we are ordinary people serving our country.
We did not ask for special consideration; we
simply put our lives on the line like every
other military person. This is the point that
cannot be ignored: we are willing to risk our
lives for this great country.

Introduction

When I retired, there was no discussion of repealing Don't Ask, Don't Tell. Three years later, a junior senator from Illinois broke onto the scene and took the world by storm, promising, among other things, to end DADT.

I thought that Senator Barack Obama's announcement that he would work on gay and lesbian issues was no more than campaign rhetoric. I knew that he would find resistance from the Republicans and that the Democrats would not make those issues a priority. Once Barack Obama became president and inherited two wars and the mess that was the US economy, I knew there was no hope for resolving gay and lesbian issues. Many in the gay community worked hard to get DADT on President Obama's radar, and so I was excited when he took up the charge. It was a relief when both houses of Congress finally passed the bill repealing DADT. That's when I decided to share my story and bring awareness to the real sacrifices made by gay military personnel of my generation and those who came before me.

In the process of writing this book, I realized that this is not just my story, but that of countless gays across the United States. So I invited some of my closest gay friends to provide insight into what military life was like for them. I learned a few things about my friends and found new respect for their sacrifices.

This book is not about pointing fingers or complaining about hardships. It is a celebration of how my friends and I served proudly despite having to hold back a major part of who we were. We had to completely separate our personal lives from our professional ones, and as you can imagine, living two lives was exhausting and often hard to manage. I hope you gain some insight into what it was like for those of us serving in silence.

On April 13, 2007, I held my retirement ceremony at Brooks City-Base in San Antonio, Texas. It was a big to-do; I wanted to go out with a bang. Ten years earlier, I had only dreamed of making it to the twenty-year mark. By all accounts, my Air Force career was a successful one, and I left behind a legacy that anyone would be proud of. In fact, my straight coworkers felt that I cut my career short. I agree, but I didn't retire because I was tired of the military. I was tired of feeling that at any moment I would get caught. I had a great career and felt I had done enough. To this day I miss being in uniform. I miss the people and the mission.

In sharing my story, I hope to answer a few questions. Some pertain to common experiences that most people go through in the military, while others might apply only to gays and lesbians. I shouldn't speak for all gays and lesbians, so let me emphasize that my story represents my experiences, and it is as factual as possible. At times I found it difficult to dig up memories from two decades ago, and I'm sure I have forgotten way more than I remember. But the most logical place to start is at the beginning.

Why I Joined the Military

My glamorous reason for joining the military was to see the world. My real reason was that I was out of options. Well, I did have one other option—to return to the small town where I was raised, which wasn't an option at all. I grew up in Bellville, Texas, a small country town an hour west of Houston. The town offered limited opportunities for young people, especially if they were black. Racism was still an issue and prevalent among many of the older white residents. I knew being gay and black in my little town left me very few options. I had so many dreams for my life, but I was dealing with a lot of demons on being black in the south and gay in a religious black family. I fought my way through high school. I wasn't the best student academically, but I did take advanced-level courses. In college, I experienced a whole new world of places and people, and I wasn't mature enough to handle it; I stayed out late and cut class. After less than a year, I knew I had to make a change.

7

I thought the Air Force would be a viable solution for my situation because my older brother had joined several years earlier. I was a nervous wreck at the recruiter's office, but joining was something I felt I had to do.

The recruiter read out loud from a questionnaire, to which I responded yes or no. There were questions about my citizenship, place of birth, education, parents, and sexuality. To be exact, there were three questions about homosexuality. *Do you consider yourself to be a homosexual?* I thought my heart was going to leap out of my chest. *Do you engage in homosexual activities? Do you associate with people who are considered homosexual?* I was convinced that the recruiter knew I was lying through my teeth. I excused myself to use the restroom and calm my nerves. *I can do this* was my mantra for the day. While washing my hands, I noticed my fingernails. Everyone who knows me will tell you that I have long, beautiful nails. This was not the day to have them on display, so I took a few minutes to bite them off. Then I gathered myself and finished the interview.

Let's say I jumped out of the pot and into the fire; at least that's how it felt to me. The recruiter told me that I had passed the entrance exam and could have my pick of jobs, except mechanics. (Frankly, I had no desire to do anything outdoors and nothing that would get dirt under my nails.) Having cleared all huddles, I was set to start my life in the military.

The first person I called was my father, who said he was glad I had joined. The military would make a man out of me, he said. Little did I know he was right—but not in the way he thought! Dad had never come right out and asked if I was gay, but he would make little comments about me needing to be "more of a man."

Basic Training Experience

While my dad and mother played a significant role in my life it was my Great Aunt Josephine Dotson who raised me. Aunt Joe would tell me all the time, "You are very special." She really wanted me to go to college, and so when I joined the Air Force, she was not happy. She felt that the military destroyed the lives of young men. It wasn't that she was unpatriotic; it's just that she had lived through the Vietnam War and seen what it did to her brothers. She also knew that her brothers had served proudly only to come back to a country where separate was not equal.

The day I left for basic training, the recruiter was to pick me up and drive me to Houston, where I would catch a bus to San Antonio. When the recruiter arrived at our house, my aunt, who suffered from angina, had a severe attack of heart palpitations. While family members were helping her, I cried at the thought of leaving. I felt as if I were killing her. Finally, my uncle forced me out the front door and into the car. I cried all the way to Houston as the recruiter assured me that I was doing the right thing. My aunt recovered, but I'm not sure she ever looked at me the same. I think she believes I was giving up on my dream of going to college.

If you are physically fit and do not have health conditions that preclude you from engaging in physical activity, you can make it through basic training. My older brother warned me the toughest part of basic training was the mind games. Remember that, he said, and you will have no problems. I recall getting off the bus and having to do the "pick-'em-up, put-'em-down" with my bags several times. I had a very old suitcase, which exploded. My clothes were everywhere, and as I tried to gather them up, the basic training instructor started shouting and spitting in my face. I remember thinking, "I cannot do this." By the time I got to my dorm room, I was exhausted and terrified, and I cried myself to sleep. After seventy-two hours I was allowed to call home. I "manned up" and told everyone I was fine.

The goal of basic training is to break you down as an individual and then build you back up as part of a team. In this I excelled, because I love team sports. I enjoy helping my teammates succeed, and to me there is nothing better than the feeling of winning as a team.

My days in basic training consisted of attending lectures, marching, and physical fitness, which usually included running, caring for military clothing, and cleaning the dorms. I received a few demerits, but overall it was smooth sailing. Among my instructor's favorite words were *fuck*, *fucker*, and *fuckin'*, and he used them a lot. He cursed at us all the time, and no matter the sentence, one of those words was involved. When I went home, I took those three words with me, because I carried with me a little part of my instructor. It caught my aunt by surprise, however, and I knew I would have to clean up my act.

I would say basic training was like being at an all-male college or boarding school. It would be a lie to say that a guy or two did not catch my eye, but, contrary to some people's notions, gay men do not want every man they see, and they do have self-control. I had no problem keeping my mind on the goal of graduating.

My flight graduated with the highest unit points for a flight. Unfortunately, we started with sixty-seven people and ended with thirty-seven. Our training instructor said it was his job to weed out the riffraff, but in the process we also lost some people who shouldn't have been kicked out of the military. I remember one man in particular who had wanted to be a chaplain's assistant, but after he woke up shaking one day, he was separated for having a nervous breakdown.

Technical Training School Experience

When I enlisted, it was impossible to secure the job I wanted. There were plenty of recruits, so there was no need to grant everyone a specific job. I joined on an open enlistment, which meant I could create a wish list of the jobs I wanted, and the Air Force would try to match my selection with its needs. Note that when you're in the military, its needs come before yours.

There were twelve in my flight with open enlistments. Of the twelve, eight were selected for Security Police, two for Recreational Services, and two for Aerospace Medicine. I'm not sure how it happened, but I was selected for Aerospace Medicine—and it was a perfect fit. I have always been a deeply spiritual person, and I enter situations knowing that God orders my footsteps. There are times when I get in the way and mess things up, and I've been told on several occasions that I can be dogmatic. As I have aged, however, I've learned to practice patience and stillness to truly understand what God has in store for me. (I also believe that God protects babies, the elderly, and fools—and I have been a bit foolish at times!) But let's get back to my story.

On June 29, 1987, I took a short ride across town to begin technical school training at Brooks Air Force Base. With Aerospace Medicine, I had entered a proud career field with a rich history. Our direct job was to care for all Air Force personnel involved in the flying mission, including pilots, navigators, astronauts, combat controllers, air traffic controllers, flight crew, and missileers. There were three major components in our career field: Aerospace and Missile Medicine, Occupational Medicine, and Physical Examinations and Standards. My career field was under an umbrella of Aerospace Medicine services that included Aerospace/Missile Medicine, Bioenvironmental Engineering, Public Health, and Aerospace Physiology. Aerospace/ Missile Medicine technicians worked directly for flight surgeons, medical doctors trained to deal with all sicknesses due to flight. We technicians managed programs involving medical waivers, hearing conservation, contact lenses, aircraft accident investigations, and medical profiles. We assisted with medical examinations and procedures, conducted the paraprofessional portion of physical medical examinations, and maintained the flight surgeons' schedules. We responded to all flight-line medical emergencies, including in-flight emergencies, deploying alongside flying units to provide routine and emergency care on the front line.

My First Duty Station

My first duty station was Zaragoza Air Base, Spain. To get there, I took my first plane ride from Houston to Dallas and then to New York. The flight to Dallas was turbulent—not a good first experience. Surprisingly, I had no flight anxiety during the rest of my trip. I slept in the LaGuardia airport, because my flight for Madrid did not leave until the following day. From Madrid I took a five-hour bus ride to Zaragoza. When I finally made it to my dorm room, I was jet-lagged and out like a light. I arrived on a Thursday, the start of Oktoberfest on the base. I did some in-processing on Friday, and by that afternoon I was enjoying the festivities on base.

For an airman, your first base is where you really learn your craft. They can teach you only so much at technical training school; the rest of your learning is on the job. I was enrolled in the Career Development Course (CDC), which is based on a series of books written by senior-ranking personnel in your career. The books are meant to provide additional

education in your career field and serve as
guides for on-the-job training. (The Aerospace
Medicine CDCs were in rewrite, so I had to
study Air Force regulations to upgrade my skill
level.) Those first two years at Zaragoza were
all about learning
aerospace medicine
and how to work in
a professional
environment.

A time-honored
military tradition
is playing jokes
on new airmen.
One of the jokes
routinely played
on males was
sending them to Supply to get "a fresh pair of
fallopian tubes." When the joke was played on
me and another new guy to the medical group,
I didn't say anything, but I remember looking
around, thinking, "That's a female body part"—I
remembered that from my anatomy and physiology
class. Obviously you can't go down to Supply to
get fallopian tubes. The other guy, however,
asked, "Okay, is there a certain size? Is
there a color?"—honestly trying to get as much
information as he could. As we headed down
to logistics, I told him I forgot something
and ducked out. Then I went back and told the
pranksters I knew what a fallopian tube is.
They called me a smart ass and told me to go
study and not say a word. Meanwhile, my fellow
airman went down to supply, where he was told,
"We only have one set left, and we gave it
to pharmacy." He then proceeded to pharmacy,
only to hear, "Oh, primary care just ordered
it." Everyone was in on the joke; no one had

to give warning that they were playing a trick on the new guy. They sent him from supply to pharmacy to primary care, and then off to the next place, everyone laughing as he made his way all over the hospital. Females, likely to know what fallopian tubes are, would be dispatched to look for sterile K-9 pee. After running all over hospital, they eventually ended up at the veterinarian area, where they would be taken out to the kennel. "Okay, just wait for Cujo to do his business," they were told, "and then you can have some sterile K-9 pee." Games like these were just little rites of passage for us airmen.

There is a special bond among airmen when they are overseas. People make more of an effort to be there for one another. When I joined my new community, I tried to fit in as well as I could. I became a CPR instructor and joined the Space Shuttle Recovery Team, and after I sang the national anthem for a change-of-command ceremony, I started going to the base gospel service and soon afterwards joined the choir, something I really enjoyed. When a female airman working in Nursing Services invited me to join the squadron's coed intramural volleyball team, it was the start of my passion for volleyball. Of all the sports I had played throughout high school, none could compare to volleyball. Eventually I made the base men's volleyball team and traveled all over Europe, playing in the Mediterranean and United States Air Forces in Europe Championships.

My supervisor and coworkers were very supportive of my extracurricular activities; I had their support because I did my job. In fact, I went above and beyond what was asked of me. Not only did I do my work, I asked if I could help others complete their assignments. I volunteered for jobs at the medical-group level that made my office look good to the commander. I stayed out of trouble, and I tried to mentor my peers. I can say without reservation that I was successful, and much of the credit goes to my first supervisor.

What I Learned from My First Supervisor

The first duty station is where you learn your job, and your supervisor plays a major role in that. My first supervisor was a great mentor who taught me how to be a professional. If I had to describe her in just a few words, I would say that Cheryl McCrary took care of her greatest resource, her people, but she also believed in completing the mission. Cheryl and I ended up becoming good friends; although she was very professional in the office, outside we were much like family. Some of that had to do with our being overseas.

Although I was obligated to work, I also wanted to see and do things outside of work. After all, when would I ever be in Spain again? "Oh come on, Cheryl," I'd say. "Just cut me a break." But in return she would say, "No break! Business comes first." At first I would pout, upset that my friend wouldn't bend the rules for me. One day when I was mad at her and wouldn't talk to her all day, she came over to me and said, "You know something? You don't have to like me to work with me."

What Cheryl said that day stuck with me. Business is business. My coworkers and I can be friends, but at the end of the day, the business has to get done. This lesson really carried me into being a non-commissioned officer (NCO) and supervisor. There were times when we could rest or play, but I was very serious about getting the mission done, and I learned that from Cheryl.

Although I looked up to Cheryl and others in the unit, the reality was they were not much older than I was. They had one advantage over me: they were on their second or third assignment. I fit in, because they were still finding their way in the military and in life. I was there when Cheryl gave birth to her son, and I spent time with her family at various on—and off-duty functions. Cheryl would even vent to me when she was upset with her husband, who worked in a different section of the hospital. As close as I felt to her, however, I did not tell her about my sexuality until years later, when she had separated from the military.

In 2004, Cheryl lost her fight with breast cancer. In the months leading up to her death, she would call me, wanting to talk only about my accomplishments. Having met and mentored me at the very beginning of my career, she now marveled at my selection to master sergeant and my completion of my Master of Social Work degree. She said she was proud that I had made the best of my time in the military and that I was finding success.

Military Women

At each assignment throughout my career, one or two women would make me the target of their affections. During the early years, I would lie and say I had a girlfriend at home. When I arrived at my first duty station in Zaragoza, I was approached by a nursing technician who, in front of other coworkers, offered to take me home for the weekend. I respectfully declined, but that would not be the last time she approached me. Over time she grew suspicious and openly questioned my sexuality. Years later, I learned that my flight commander had told her that he didn't care if I slept with cows—I was his best worker. I was glad to hear my flight commander felt that way, but it was concerning to know such conversations were happening.

At every duty station, there was always a woman or two who would come on to me. I think women love the closeness they feel with a gay man. It's almost as if the man is one of the girls; there's a level of intimacy. Women see the male body parts and start believing it could work out. I felt stuck, because I could not tell these women that I'm gay. As much as I would have liked to entrust my secret to someone I considered a friend, I could not take the chance that she would betray my confidence. The key was never to provide proof I was gay, although I'm not saying that no one ever suspected it.

During my second assignment, in Aviano, Italy, I drew the attention and attraction of a medical administration technician. I actually liked this woman; she was good at her job, full of life, and fun to be around. The problem was that she put me on the spot in front of our coworkers. There was a trend developing that would follow me my entire career.

Twice during my last assignment, my sexuality was called into question. At that time I was with the Office of the USAF Surgeon General, Air Force Medical Support Agency, Population

Health Support Division at Brooks City-Base, Texas. I spent seven years with this group and was very close with my military and civilian coworkers.

The first situation involved a lovely coworker who reminded me of my paternal grandmother and aunts. I felt close to this lady; we shared a love of God, singing, pinochle, and cooking. During our seven years as coworkers, we sang together at division holiday parties and even performed the national anthem together during change-of-command and promotion ceremonies. Coworkers loved our cooking and often challenged us to outdo each other with the dishes we created for various functions. We partnered up during pinochle and spades card games, and when I retired from the military I spent three days at her home prior to moving to Houston. Somewhere along the way, my friend fell in love with me. All I could think was, "Oh no, not again."

It started with her innocent comment about how I would make someone a good husband; then it moved to, "If I were twenty years younger . . ." (She is one year younger than my mother.) My first response was to thank her for the compliment and try to move on, but eventually it became a bit uncomfortable; she began looking at me as if she were ready to eat me up. As I was in the process of retiring from the Air Force and moving, it would have been easy to overlook the situation. The problem was, I really liked this person, and I believed our friendship was worth saving. So I broke with normal protocol and disclosed my sexuality in hopes of defusing the situation. She told me that God could change me and that she would pray for me. Soon afterwards, I moved away and limited my contact with her. When I finally spoke with her, she said she understood my feelings and just wanted to be friends.

The problem is that her eyes said something totally different. When I went back to San Antonio for a visit, I took her to a play as thanks for helping me collect data during my dissertation. During the play, she tried to hold hands with me. I was deeply saddened by the incident and have not been able to reach out to her again, although I do keep up with her through friends.

The second situation caught me totally off guard. Near the end of my military career, one of my coworkers, Senior Master Sergeant Robert "Spence" Spencer, confronted me about my sexuality. He is now retired, but at the time he was the senior enlisted superintendent for the Population Health Support Division. Through our many visits to various Air Force bases, Spence and I developed a friendship that reminds me of my relationship with my brothers: "He thinks he can tell me what to do." One moment we were solving complex problems, and the next moment we were at each other's throats. Ours is the deepest friendship I have ever had with a straight person while on active duty.

While we were attending the National Association of Black Social Workers' Conference in Houston, Spence finally confronted me. (He had been dropping little hints over the previous month to gauge my comfort level.) "Is there something you want to tell me?" he asked. Remember, my motto is never to provide proof, so I played stupid. Still, he persisted. I said, "I'm sure I do not know what you're talking about." I wasn't nervous; I had been down this road before. But there was something different this time—maybe it was the fact that I was nearing retirement, or maybe it was the closeness I felt with Spence. It took him a couple of minutes to put me at ease. Finally, I said, "Yes."

Now my heart felt like it was about to leap out of my chest. Up until then, I had never confided in or disclosed my sexuality to anyone who was in a position to hurt me. I felt very vulnerable.

Spence smiled and said he was upset that he had to force the truth out of me. I explained that it was a burden I had never shared before, and he understood. In fact, my revelation actually drew us closer. Now I had someone with whom I could relax and be myself—and that was important, because I spent a lot of time with Spence. We worked together, went fishing and camping, and attended movies, plays, and musicals. Some of my friends call Spence my "boyfriend" because we spend so much time together. Really, ours is a wonderful platonic relationship, forged by our mutual interests. I am happy to say that Spence and I are still friends—no, more than friends. Brothers.

After retiring from the Air Force, I was a social work case manager with Kelsey-Seybold Clinic in Houston. I was assigned to a department where all but one employee was female, and during my first tour of the office I saw the women's heads pop up from their cubicles—it looked like a game of Whac-a-Mole. Around my fourth day of work, my female coworkers dispatched a representative to my cube to give me the third degree. She was one of the older ladies in the office, and she wasn't shy about asking direct questions. My coworkers wanted to know if I had a girlfriend, was married, or was gay. One of the wonderful things about being retired from the military is that I no longer have to hide; I can choose to disclose my sexuality to my female coworkers so they can stop wasting their time. I do not broadcast my sexuality to the world, but it is nice to have the option. By the way, I shared my sexuality with the ladies and they accepted me with open arms.

First Time Going to a Gay Bar in the Military

When you are gay, you want to be around other gay people once in a while, so this means going to places like gay bars and clubs. Every military base keeps a list of establishments that are off-limits, and every gay bar is usually on that list—the official reason, usually, is that it is "a known haven for drugs." As you can imagine, anyone caught at an off-limits establishment is in a tough situation. At my very first duty station, Zaragoza, I lived in fear of being caught, so for the first six months I went only to work, the gym, the dining hall, church, and my dorm room. I usually stayed away from anyone I thought might be gay, and if another man approached me, I assumed it was a set-up. Overall, I was very mistrusting of people; you really had to put the heavy moves on me in order for me to let down my guard.

When I first signed into the base, I met an older man named Dennis, who had returned to Spain for a second tour. Six months later, after staying in virtual confinement, I ventured out to one of the local gay bars. I felt like fresh meat—the music and conversation paused as I walked through the door. Then I spotted Dennis and thought I would die. I hid in a corner and tried to stay out of sight, but he eventually made his way over and started a conversation. I was approached many times throughout the night. I ended up having a good time, and I walked out with ten phone numbers. It was a completely new experience for me—coming from a small, racially charged town and then going to Europe, where they adored my black skin. I thought I had died and gone to heaven.

Over time, I learned a few tips to keep the Office of Special Investigations off my back. I always parked away from the bar and looked for back door exits in case of emergencies. An emergency would be a known undercover security policemen or OSI agent entering the bar. I felt it was good practice to know these people by sight and also to know what type of vehicles they drove. (I learned years later that it wouldn't have helped; OSI brought in agents from other bases to do undercover work.) While my close friends and I were careful, and I cannot say the same for others.

HIV/AIDS in Military

Taking an HIV test has always caused me to have heart palpitations. When I was in the military, there was a three-week wait to get results. The waiting itself caused a lot of anxiety, not to mention my fear of how the military would react if I tested positive. That would mean dealing with the Office of Public Health, which included interviews, and partner notification. This caused greater anxiety.

Although I didn't have to tell the public health technician anything, going through the interview would be unbearable, especially because I worked closely with this office.

Working in Aerospace Medicine meant I conducted physicals for all military personnel on the base, clearing them for deployment, assignments, and entrance into the military. This put me directly in the path of their HIV test results. Although we used code on the paperwork to reveal a person's HIV status, it wasn't private by any means; everyone in the hospital knew who on base was HIV-positive.

One of my worst memories from Zaragoza is of a young black guy who lived with his sister and taught dance on the base. I would see him out at clubs, and although we weren't friends, we knew each other. In 1988, he decided to join the military. I worked in physical examinations and standards, so I had to conduct his physical. One day I showed up at work and everyone was acting as though they had lost their minds. This young man's HIV test had come back positive. I had been on the base for more than a year, and this was the first HIV-positive lab result that I knew of.

Shortly thereafter, the young man lost his job on the base. He was escorted from the premises, and I had to sit in the back of an ambulance and tell him he couldn't join the military because he was HIV-positive. (This was before triple medical therapies for HIV/AIDS; surviving the disease wasn't as common as it is today.) I was scared because this young man knew that I was gay. I was also terrified because I was having sex and sometimes didn't use protection, which made me fear for my own life. This hit to close to home, and it should have been a reality check. I was twenty years old with a lot to learn.

I dated someone in San Antonio for about eight months in 1995, and I'll admit that I did not always use a condom. I had every intention of doing so, but sometimes it just didn't happen. After we broke up, I found out that he had been sleeping around, and it soon came out that he had slept with someone who was HIV-positive. When I confronted my ex, he would not admit to having slept around or to being HIV-positive, but I noticed that he had lost a significant amount of weight. Naturally, I was beside myself with worry. In 2001, I received a letter ordering me to report to the hospital for a physical. After the exam was finished, I was told to report to the lab. I went home instead.

In December 2003, I was on an educational leave of absence from the military, completing my master's degree in social work, when my commander called and said, "Come to my office, and be in uniform." When I reported to her office, she ordered me to report to the clinic to complete the blood work portion of my physical. I completed the blood work and drove home, where I cried for a little while and tried to come up with a plan to deal with the military if I were to test positive. It was ten days before I was due to graduate with my master's.

The Air Force doesn't contact you if it's good news, and getting bad news can take a long three weeks. During that time I didn't get a lot of sleep and I tried to keep busy with things like school work, but when things got quiet at night, I was alone with my thoughts. I woke up one day and three months had gone

by. I knew my test was negative. Naturally, I
pledged never to have sex again.

The Office of Special Investigations

As cautious as I was about protecting my
sexual orientation, I still had two encounters
with the OSI. The first incident happened
shortly after I moved from Zaragoza, Spain,
to Aviano, Italy. My friend Dennis was under
investigation and it was my misfortune that
he was being watched. When I sent him a card
signed, "I miss you, love you, and need to
hear your voice," it was intercepted—and it
set off a firestorm.

I was told to report to OSI and wear my
military service dress. I had no idea why I
was being ordered there, but I was terrified
all the same. I was read my rights, shown a
photocopy of the card, and then, believe it
or not, I was interrogated under a bright
light, just like in the movies. I remember
thinking that I would never be able to talk
my way out of this one. The OSI agent started
by saying that he knew I spent a lot of time
with Dennis; this I did not deny. Then he used
several approaches to get me to confess.

First he attacked the content on my card.
Straight men don't talk to each that way, he
said. I held my ground, stating that I was not
taught to love my male friends differently
than I do my female friends—which is true. I
am who I am, and I make no apologies for it.
After a while came the second attack, as the
agent assured me that there was nothing wrong
with being gay. I was supposed to relax and
agree so he could turn it around and say, "But

being gay is not conducive to military life." Instead, I stayed the course and provided no information he could use against me. His last attack was also his key mistake: he told me that Dennis had confessed that we had been lovers. When he said that, I knew he was grasping at straws. I knew that my friend would not make a false statement, especially one that implicated me. I also knew that even if he had broken and admitted to being gay, he wouldn't admit to something that wasn't true. With no proof against me, the case was dropped.

That incident put me on the straight and narrow. I went to work, church, the gym, and my dorm room; that was my life for six months. After seven months had passed, I thought I would go crazy. I had a good friend stationed about two hours away with NATO, so I caught a train and we hit a gay club about five hours from base. I finally settled into a normal social rhythm, which included going out with gay friends.

My second brush with OSI came in October 1995, when I was leaving Minot Air Force Base, North Dakota, to go to the United States Air Force School of Aerospace Medicine at Brooks Air Force Base in San Antonio. While I was out-processing from Minot, I was informed that I was under investigation for being gay. The movers had found among my belongings some pictures of me hugging another man; they were in a box that I had packed and taped. I had broken my cardinal rule: Provide no proof.

My mother was now living with me, and my income was her sole source of support. I was terrified; I knew I had no defense against what was coming my way. I had checked out of base housing and we were staying with friends.

OSI's new policy was to turn over any initial investigation to the commanding officer of the person in question.

When my investigation was assigned to a lieutenant from my squadron, I knew I was in hot water, because we did not have a good rapport. In fact, we did not care for each other at all. The lieutenant began by asking me to turn over the pictures—which was confusing, as I had been told that the military had the pictures. I didn't know what to say other than, "There are no pictures."

Several days later I was called to the first sergeant's office. He was new to the group, which meant I didn't know him well. He said he had recently lost a friend to AIDS, and he told me to be careful and not put myself in jeopardy. He had some sage advice for me as I embarked on a very public position as an instructor. My new position was very public and would require me to be more protective of my secret. He finally told me that the case was closed and that I was free to go. All I can say is, there is a God, and he is good all the time! Note: I never got my pictures back; I left town before the first sergeant could change his mind.

This incident was a wake-up call that set me back on the path of being diligent about protecting my personal life. You might say that I knew the risk, and had the outcome been administrative discharge, I would have gotten what I deserved. But this one incident does not reflect my overall character or achievements throughout my military career.

Life in the Military before Don't Ask,

Don't Tell

Before DADT, the military actively pursued gays and lesbians. We called this pursuit the "witch hunts"; the military treated us as though we were criminals. Conducting physical exams on people being administratively discharged made me face this reality. I processed people leaving the military for adultery, drugs, theft, writing bad checks—and for being gay. Some gay airmen actually went to jail for fraudulent enlistment; if the military could show they were gay prior to enlisting, they had committed fraud because, technically, they had lied about it. It was sad seeing them lumped in with the rest. The military treated them like they were criminals, but I treated them as fairly as possible. When I met with them, for example, I would make the military escort leave, and for the hour or two I was with them, I would try to make them feel as comfortable as I could. Before Don't Ask, Don't Tell, it was a very aggressive atmosphere.

Life under Don't Ask, Don't Tell

After DADT became law, the military officially stopped its aggressive pursuit of gays and lesbians, but there still seemed to be a lot of gay people facing discharge. To tell you the truth, I did not feel any less fearful about being found out. The bottom line? I still had to be careful at all times.

Accomplishments in the Military

I have always found it hard to write about my accomplishments, but I think a chapter outlining my stellar performance over twenty years in the military is warranted.

I got my work ethic from my great aunt Josephine Dotson, who worked tirelessly serving her family, church, and community. I learned from her selflessness, which was on constant display, and excellence and integrity were also part of my home training. Those lessons would prepare me for a career in the Air Force, whose core values include excellence in all we do, integrity first, and service before self. I loved working in teams and having a specific mission; I was thrilled by the fact that the work I did was tied to the larger mission of the Air Force. As an aerospace medicine technician, my primary mission was prevention and intervention, keeping the base healthy and returning personnel to duty quickly following illness.

I love innovation, so I'm always looking for ways to make programs and processes work better. Initially I embraced this innovative approach because of my upbringing and because I feared someone discovering my secret. If I was a valued member of the team, I thought, it wouldn't matter if my supervisor or commander learned I was gay. Over time, though, I looked for innovative opportunities because it was second nature—I really enjoyed making positive change. I am so proud of my career and my accomplishments. I would like to outline a few of them:

1. Zaragoza Air Base, Spain

a. I implemented the first Coronary Artery Risk Evaluation (CARE) program in the United States Air Forces in Europe (USAFE). I brought the program online six months ahead of schedule and was singled out for recognition by an evaluation team from Headquarters USAFE.

b. I was a member of the Zaragoza Air Base Space Shuttle Recovery Team.

c. As a member of the Zaragoza base men's volleyball team, I represented the base at the Air Force Mediterranean and all-USAFE Volleyball Championships. In 1989 I was selected to the Mediterranean volleyball all-star team.

d. In 1989, I was awarded the Air Force Achievement Medal for exceptional performance.

2. Aviano Air Base, Italy

a. From 1989 to 1991, I was a member of the Aviano Air Base gospel choir, representing the base in concerts and festivals throughout Italy.

b. From 1990 to 1991, I was a member of the base men's volleyball team, representing the base at the Mediterranean and USAFE volleyball championships and being selected to the Mediterranean volleyball all-star team.

c. In 1989, I was awarded the Air Force Commendation Medal for meritorious service.

3. Minot Air Force Base, North Dakota
   a. From 1992 to 1995, I was a member of the Minot Air Force Base men's volleyball team, representing the base at the North Dakota Outdoor Games. From 1994 to 1995, I served as player/coach for the base.
   b. I served as a member of the base Search and Rescue Team, with medical responsibilities including search-and-rescue missions for downed pilots during wartime and humanitarian search-and-rescue missions for the state of North Dakota.
   c. In 1993, I was awarded the Esprit-de-Corps peer-selected award during Airman Leadership School.
   d. In 1994, I received the NATO Medal and the Armed Forces Service Medal for my participation in Deny Flight and Provide Hope for Kosovo.
   e. In 1995, I was awarded the Air Force Commendation Medal for meritorious service.

4. Brooks Air Force Base, Texas
   a. In 1995, I was hand-picked to become an aerospace medicine instructor at USAF School of Aerospace Medicine. During my tenure I achieved the level of master instructor and served as non-commissioned officer in charge over the apprentice and advanced aerospace medicine courses and the hearing conservation and recertification courses.
   b. In 1997, I was selected as the non-commissioned officer (NCO) of the

quarter for USAF School of Aerospace Medicine.

c. In 1998, I received the Air Force Achievement Medal for helping reduce the student attrition rate in the aerospace medicine apprentice course.

d. In 1998, I received the Aerospace Medicine Team Award for educational contributions to the career field.

e. From 1996 to 2005, I was a member of the Brooks Air Force Base men's volleyball team. 1999 to 2005, I served as player/coach for the base team. I also represented Brooks AFB at the Air Force Materiel Command (AFMS) Men's Volleyball Championships. From 1997 to 2005, I was selected to the AFMS men's all-star volleyball team.

f. In 2000, I received the Air Force Commendation Medal for meritorious service while stationed at the USAF School of Aerospace Medicine.

5. Office of the USAF Surgeon General/Air Force Medical Support Agency

a. In 2000, I received the Air Force Achievement Medal from the USAF Surgeon General for outstanding performance during the Primary Care  Optimization Quick Start course.

b. In 2002, I was awarded the Brooks City-Base Commander's Trophy for outstanding performance during 2001.

c. In 2002, I was selected as the USAF Surgeon
   General's NCO of the year for 2001.
d. In 2002, I was selected as the Pentagon
   USAF NCO of the year for 2001.
e. In 2003, I was selected as senior NCO of
   the third quarter.
f. In 2004, I received the Meritorious
   Service Medal for commendable service
   while stationed with the Air Force Medical
   Support Agency/Population Health Support
   Division.

I look back over my career and feel a sense
of pride not just in my accomplishments, but
also in the fact that I served in a way that
honors my family's rich military history. My
father, my twin brother, my older brother, and
I have a combined ninety-six years of military
service, representing the Air Force, the navy,
and the army.

Knowing that one day I would have to leave
the Air Force, I pursued my education at night;
I had seen so many people separate or retire
from the Air Force with no real game plan
for their future. It took me a while to get
started, but once I was focused, I was a man
on a mission.

1. In 1996, I received an Associate of Allied
   Sciences Health degree from the Community
   College of the Air Force.
2. In 1999, I received an Associate of Allied
   Science in Instructor Technology and Military
   Sciences degree from the Community College
   of the Air Force.
3. In 1999, I completed the USAF School of
   Aerospace Medicine teaching practicum.

4. In 2001, I received a bachelor's degree in liberal arts from Excelsior College.
5. In 2003, I received a Master of Social Work degree from Our Lady of the Lake University, graduating with a 3.957 grade point average.
6. In 2003, I was inducted into Phi Alpha, social work national honor society.

7. In 2009, I received a Doctor of Health Administration degree from the University of Phoenix, graduating with a 3.55 GPA.

I completed all but two years of my education
while on active duty, so I spent many nights
and weekends attending class. I emphasize this
fact because it shows that I never let my
work and dedication to the military falter. In
fact, in the middle of completing my master's
degree I was selected as the Pentagon's NCO of
the year.

Protecting My Career

As careful as I was to protect my career
from my private life, for years I looked over
my shoulder, worried that the military would
"catch" me. These feelings finally subsided as
I got older, more mature, and more comfortable.
Usually around the second year I was on a
base, people would start questioning me about
my relationships. As a young airman, I felt
the need to make up stories about having a
girlfriend. As I got older, however, I had a
different attitude; I had no problem telling
people that I would share only what I wanted
them to know—everything else was none of their
business. If a man asked me if I was gay, I
would get angry and return the question with
"Why, are you asking me out?" When he would
say no, I would follow with, "Then why are you
asking me about my sexuality?" I would put him
on the defense, while his goal had been to put
me on the defensive. It took me a long time to
stand up for myself and not allow people to
back me into a corner.

When I had just started work on my Doctor
of Health Administration degree, I ran into
an army captain whom I would see from time

to time at Borders. This time we spoke for about an hour, talking about work and school, and finally she said, "I'm going to ask you a question. Do you mind?" When I told her to go ahead, she asked if I was gay. "You have some nerve," I said, "and that is not any of your business." Then I stopped talking to her and went back to my studies. I was so angry; we had only known each other for an hour, and she was digging for personal information. I was no longer timid about putting people in their place.

It was hard to have a long-term relationship because I couldn't fully open up. I dated, but I couldn't keep a relationship. I remember going out with my boyfriend at the time, along with my cousin and her boyfriend, and during the movie, while my cousin and her boyfriend were all over each other, my boyfriend put his hand on my stomach and I almost lost it. I didn't know my cousin's boyfriend—I knew only that he was in the army reserves—but he knew I was active-duty military. It was a delicate situation.

Would I serve again?

Although the military changed my life for the better, it wasn't always easy. Not only was I investigated twice, but I also was separated from my family. There was a time when my two brothers and I were all on different continents, and for one ten-year stretch, I didn't see my twin brother at all. On the other hand, military life helped me learn to get along with many types of people. As a new enlistee, I didn't have a lot of experience

with people of other races. I had grown up
in a town where I was subjected to racism,
and because of that I didn't have a favorable
opinion of some people. But in the military, I
learned to treat people for who they are.

I propose everyone serve in the military
for two years; in return, receive tuition to
attend a four-year state college. My first two
years in the military allowed me to grow up,
and I know for a fact that I would not be "Dr.
McFarland" if I had not joined the military.
Traveling the world and working at various
levels within the Air Force medical system was
invaluable. My experiences brought me to where
I am today, and I wouldn't trade them for the
world.

If given the chance, however, I would serve
as an openly gay man. I would have loved to
share my sexuality with whomever I wanted and
bring a partner wherever I wanted. I would
have loved to serve in the military and not
have the burden of constantly looking over my
shoulder.

Interview with Kenneth N. (Kenny) Brooks

Kenny is one of my oldest gay friends in the military. I met him in the summer of 1990 at a gay club in Italy. I walked into the club and noticed an American guy dancing—it was a sight to behold. Dressed in jeans and cowboy boots, Kenny would "drop it like it's hot" and then go down into the splits. (Anyone who knows Kenny knows I'm telling the truth. A mutual friend introduced us, and we've been lifelong friends ever since. Our careers have moved us all over the world, but we've always been able to reconnect. An interesting coincidence: Kenny and I were promoted to technical sergeant and master sergeant during the same promotion cycles.

In 1994, Kenny told me he wanted to separate from the Air Force and move to Washington DC. When I asked him if he had finished his four-year degree or saved enough money to pay his bills, his answer was no—and he stayed in. The rest is history.

Kenny was my road buddy; he and I use to go clubbing together in Italy. Kenny often worked weekend shifts, so whenever he told me he had a free weekend, I would say, "It sounds like an Alcazar night." (Alcazar was one of the

Italian gay night clubs we frequented.) Kenny
and I were young, alive, and living in Italy,
and our time there served as a coming-of-age
experience for me. I learned about love,
relationships, loyalty, and manhood, and I
knew Kenny and I would be lifelong friends.

I have a deep admiration for Kenny and how
he served his military career. Kenny was a
straight-shooter; you always knew where you
stood with him. People liked that about Kenny
and found it easy to be around him. He also was
very comfortable just being himself. Remember
how I first saw Kenny dancing at the gay club?
Well, he would dance the same way at the base
club. I would be shocked, but other people
loved it. All the female airmen would join him
on the dance floor and have a ball. I wouldn't
have gotten away with half the things that
Kenny did. In a way, Kenny was able to hide in
plain sight because of his personality and the
effect he had on people. He hasn't changed in
the twenty-plus years I've known him. Here is
my interview with Kenny.

Why did you join the military?

Before I joined the military I attended
Winston-Salem State University for one year and
then transferred to East Carolina University
during my second year. I was a computer science
major with significant student loans, and I
started getting bored and frustrated. I had
relatives who were in the Air Force, which
gave me the idea that joining would allow me
to make money and finish school. So I went to
a recruiter and signed up.

The first thing my father said when I joined was that the military would make a man out of me. Ignoring his ignorance, I decided that this was what I had to do if I wanted to go somewhere. I had spent every summer since ninth grade working with my uncle, who restored wood floors in New York. I would look around these private homes and see the material things the homeowners had worked hard for—their business clothes in their freshly finished closets—and I decided I had to do something to attain this life style. Growing up in rural eastern North Carolina, I would stare up into the night sky and watch the aircraft flying overhead with their red and green lights (identifying the right and left sides, although I didn't know that at the time), and I remember thinking, "Wow, they must be important people going to important places to do important things."

I was young and naïve, but I knew that I *had* to get out of that village. When you know you're different—when you think differently than everyone else, when you want to do things differently than everyone else, when you behave differently than everyone else—you know that you need to leave and find people like you. The world is a big place, and I needed to see more of it.

Why did you choose the Air Force?

I originally thought about joining the army, because I had family serving in the army, but I changed my mind and joined the Air Force. I didn't want to join the marines or the navy; being out to sea never crossed my mind. I figured the Air Force operated more like a corporation, and once I saw a lot of cadets walking around, I decided I would give it a try.

Tell me about your Military Entrance Processing Station (MEPS) experience.

My experience was a normal one. I "walked like a duck," underwent all the tests, and did what I was supposed to do. I remember someone looking over my records and telling me that I should have joined the army, but I said I had already made my choice. Maybe my experience wasn't so normal, I recall a recruiter talking about his body parts and sexual experiences. I glanced over to see what he was talking about, and he asked if I was gay. I just stared at him. Once I had my hand up and was sworn in, I felt like I was a man and this was how it was supposed to be.

Tell me about your basic training experience.

The final night before basic training, my cousin Vanessa, with whom I grew up, buried her mother. I drove up to Raleigh, North Carolina, that evening and flew out the next day. My mother had wanted me to finish college first, but because I didn't want more student loans, I knew I was doing the right thing.

When I started basic training at Lackland Air Force Base in San Antonio, I wasn't anxious or sad, mainly because I knew what I had to do: follow the mandatory instructions of the training instructors. But if you had grown up with my mother, you'd realize that the orders they barked out were a rehash of what my mother would tell my siblings and me. Mere child's play! I also remember being happy while driving to the base because I was looking forward to shopping on the weekends. There I was on the bus, picking out which stores in the mall I would visit during my days off. Now you know why they say ignorance is bliss.

After I arrived at the basic training site I had to deal with the "pick-'em-up, put-'em-down" of my bags, which I thought was asinine. Then, for some reason, the training instructor started walking towards me. I wondered what he was going to do; I had been following his simple instruction. My saving grace was a fair-complexioned African-American guy whose purple and hot-pink plaid pants completely diverted the TI's attention away from me. To quote Miss Sofia from *The Color Purple*, "There is a God!"

I never cried, but I watched everyone else cry. I had already experienced being on my own

from living five hours from home in college. This is likely why it was fairly easy for me to be away from home.

My basic training lasted from November 1986 to January 1987. The holidays are when the majority of these "macho" men would cry and pine for home. Hmmmm . . . imagine being in combat with *that* crew during a holiday! My gaydar wasn't as fine-tuned then as it is now, but in retrospect, I'm pretty sure I wasn't the only gay one in the bunch.

I flew under the radar at basic training. I followed instructions and stayed out of the line of fire. Besides, the residential "house mouse," the TI's assistant, was a *lot* more effeminate than I was. If *he* wasn't a gay suspect, then I couldn't be. Also during basic, one of the guys I had arrived with claimed to have three testicles, and I witnessed another guy drop to his knees to count them personally. Yep, the guy on his knees said to our flight, it was true: Airman Basic "Snuffy" did indeed have three testicles. And they were gonna pick *me* out of the bunch for being gay?

I was selected for a top-secret clearance, so there were quite a few events and activities that I didn't participate in because I was busy filling out paperwork. I even missed marching in my graduation because there was more paper to fill out. I didn't mind at the time; it was too costly for my family to drive from North Carolina to Texas, anyway.

I do remember a few funny incidents from basic training. They didn't have my tennis shoe size, so I was given shoes one size too small, but I never complained; I didn't want to draw attention. Once when I was standing in formation, a song popped into my head, and I forgot where I was for a moment and started dancing in place before quickly regaining my military composure and falling back into formation. Another morning I ran downstairs without my glasses and ended up getting into the wrong formation. (It was pitch-black outside.) All of a sudden, the formation started to do

a side-step maneuver that I had never done
before with my formation, but since the step
had a rhythm, and I have rhythm, I was able to
follow along. After we stopped doing the step,
and since it was still dark outside, I quickly
tip-toed over to my own flight. Luckily, we
were side-by-side that morning. Other than
those few little things, I steered clear of
trouble and went about the routine of taking
basic training one day at a time.

Tell me about your first duty station.

My first duty station was Aviano Air Base,
Italy, where I spent three of my most glorious
Air Force years. In basic training I was able to
create a wish list of places I would like to be
stationed. Aviano was my first choice. My time
away from home when I was in college or living
with relatives in New York City helped prepare
me for being on my own in Italy, but I still had
a lot to learn about other cultures. I really
grew up at my first duty station, and being in
Italy gave me a worldly perspective on things.

When I first arrived there, I just tried to
fit in like everyone else. On my first foray
into the village of Aviano, I went with our
admin troop, Emerald. She took me to a club
called Etta's. That was the place where the
black folk liked to hang out, so that's where
we went. Afterwards, we went up to a club
called Quarterway (a quarter of the way up the
mountain). While observing the scene there,
I was approached by a woman who told me that
she wanted to have my baby. I thought it was
hilarious, but I ignored her.

I didn't attend a gay club in Italy until I had been in country for six or seven months. My initial year or so in Italy—around 1988 or 1989—we in the Weather Station were having a discussion about gays in the military, and one of my senior bosses looked me directly in the eyes and said that he had no problem working with gay people, that some of his best workers were gay. I knew that he knew. But I only responded, "Well, that's good to know," and kept moving forward. After all that, my life on base went on without too much drama; I continued to do my job to the best of my ability.

Really, the only problem I ever had while stationed in Italy involved a base security policeman who would harass me whenever I came through the gate. He had to check my ID card, but he acted as though he didn't want to touch it. I reported him to the Social Actions Office, but he ended up being kicked out of the Air Force for fraudulently enlisting in the military. The ironic thing is that he was friends with a friend of mine who was clearly, recognizably gay. Oh well, life goes on—and so did I.

I met some of my best Italian and American friends, both straight and gay, while stationed in Italy. My straight friends wanted me to hang out with them so they could have a good time, as well. I loved to dance and had no problem getting everyone on the dance floor. I wasn't a party animal, but I knew how to have a good time.

What did you learn from your first supervisor?

I do not recall learning much of anything from my first supervisor; I remember a lot of joking around. I was self-motivated, so the lack of guidance from my supervisor was not a problem. Completing my career development courses was all about learning the most that I could, and I saw it as a competition with other airmen. Everyone wanted to outdo everyone else, and your supervisor expected you to outscore your peers.

Something I learned from experience was always to watch my back. I had noticed that some of my accomplishments were recorded on a roommate's or coworker's performance report instead of mine. (I knew this because I was shown their performance reports.) When I asked how this happened, I was told that that's how things were done. In short, I learned to watch my back and always document my work.

Tell me about military women.

At my first base in Italy, one female in particular kept telling me that she wanted me to be the father of her kids, but obviously nothing ever came of it. I would keep people at a distance, which I considered to be a gift to them. I would never let a woman get close enough to want to be with me. I was more about just having a good time.

Let me point out that I did not cut female airmen any slack—not because I was gay, but because they all wear a uniform. I would help lift something heavy, but I felt that we are all the same and we were all there together. Females had to be proficient in all job-related tasks, just like their male counterparts. I surely wasn't going to fail an inspection because of someone else. If the men were going to get sweaty, so should the women.

Tell me about your first time going to a gay bar while in the military.

I started venturing out to gay bars at my first duty station. I was in Italy for six months when a friend took me to a bar called Edle's. I remember seeing my friend Stephan there, although we weren't friends at the time. A short time later I was formally introduced to Stephan, and we've stay friends to this day. The first gay bar I went to in Italy was called Alcazar—only the second gay club I had ever visited. As the oldest sibling in my family and having come from a small town, I had never really gotten to venture out before.

Tell me about your experience with HIV/ AIDS in the military.

Hmmmmm . . . HIV/AIDS in the military. Those were the words no one *ever* wanted to hear while serving on active duty. Every year, depending upon your time on station or whether you were due to move to another base or go on a deployment, you were tested for HIV. Some unfortunate souls would discover at this crucial time that they indeed were HIV-positive. And as if contracting the disease weren't bad enough, as an active duty member you were required to let your commander know about your HIV status when you got to any new base. Your commander was the only one who needed to know; it was no one else's place to know. In the base hospital, your medical records were filed along with everyone else's, with no special markings to indicate your HIV status. One of the *worst* things you had to endure was the verification that your HIV status was up to date whenever you made a medical appointment. So those people working in the clinic who didn't know your status? Well, now they did. According to HIPAA, this information was to remain private, but we all know human nature. Rumors do spread beneath the radar.

During my tenure in the Air Force, which began in the mid-eighties as the HIV/AIDS epidemic was really taking off, those letters were like a death sentence to your military career. And if you happened to be stationed overseas at the time, well, once your diagnosis was determined, the military did not give you time to pack up your household goods or say good-bye to anyone. You were hurriedly flown back to the States, to Wilford Hall Medical Center in San Antonio, the Air Force's main hospital for treating HIV/AIDS. This left friends to pack your household goods. (Normally, it was your first sergeant who got to go through your personal effects, although most likely, he or she didn't volunteer for the job.) Such a hurried move back to the States always caused whispering on base; when you're stationed overseas, you tend to be closer to your military brothers and sisters than when you are stationed stateside.

I remember being a young airman stationed in Italy and going to take an HIV test. Well, in the military, no news in good news, and that's exactly how you would discover that you were negative—no one from the clinic would call. But this particular time, one of my earliest supervisors, who was known to be a prankster, "jokingly" yelled to me across the office that the base clinic had called and that my HIV test had come back positive. At first, I froze in place, but then, after a few seconds, I countered that it hadn't—and if it had, they wouldn't have told him. Welcome to the Air Force! Still, I continued to be nervous every time I took an HIV test. There were times I didn't really stress about them too much, especially if I hadn't been on the dating scene, but once that changed, it was nail biting time again.

I did have two friends, who were also friends with each other, who tested positive within a week of one another. One of the results I could understand, since the man was *very* promiscuous, but the other left me flabbergasted. I remember telling a friend that I was swearing off sex forever, but as we know, forever is a long time, and that old feeling comes roaring back. I also wondered how two of my other friends could sleep with everybody and everything and *not* be HIV-positive. It just didn't seem fair.

One day after I was back stateside, a close friend called me. "I'm dying," he said, without even saying hello. "We're all born to die," I replied. But he said no, he was HIV-positive—he had gotten it from his current boyfriend. Although my friend was monogamous in the relationship and so had decided to forego protection, his boyfriend had been sleeping around without using protection, unbeknownst to my friend. I asked myself, How could someone so smart be so stupid?

But we all know how love can drive us to do insane things. In my quest to replace the feeling I had had in a previous relationship (a relationship I now realize was one-sided), I became very promiscuous. It's just amazing how numb you can become when your heart has been broken—putting yourself in danger for a simple touch from a stranger, a touch that can take you back to what you thought you had. During this "blind" period in my life, a friend and I took a Caribbean cruise, during which, suffice it to say, I partook way too much of the alcoholic beverages, and I met a kind gentleman. After all was said and done, when I returned to base I was selected to take an HIV test. *Nervous* is an understatement for how I felt—not just about the possibility of having the disease, but also about letting people in the military know.

Being HIV-positive in the military can make you feel as though you're no longer an asset to your country. After all, you can't deploy to any of the foreign conflicts that are occurring; you can't even get stationed outside the United States. But what a lot of people fail to realize is that the same rules apply if you have diabetes, cancer or severe asthma. A point of fact is that I myself am not HIV-positive. And I have to give glory to God for that fact, because I know that I've made intimate mistakes. As I've gotten older, my rule of thumb has been to treat all intimate partners as if they are HIV-positive.

Any experiences with the Office of Special Investigations?

I remember the behavior of a gay airman who was really messy when it came to his sex life. He had gay porn in his locker on base, metal penis rings, leather wrist bands, and so on. He would also rent fancy cars and drive them around base. He would show up to work out of

uniform, wearing a gray beret (which was not
authorized), and sometimes he smelled of urine.
One day he was sitting at work when he overheard
that there was going to be a raid on his dorm.
He automatically left his desk to hide all his
things, but when he reached his room, Security
Police were waiting for him; they had noticed
he had left his desk immediately, which caused
suspicion. At that point they went through
his locker and found the gay paraphernalia.
When his case was reviewed by legal, however,
the ruling was that because he wasn't in any
of the pictures or videos, he was protected
under the First Amendment; just because he was
looking at this material didn't mean he was
gay. They were able to kick him out of the
military anyway because of other things—the
uniform, financial irresponsibility, poor work
performance, and so on—but it was because of
the porn that the push was on to get him out.
I was worried because he had actually run over
to my room to tell me about the raid, and I
was afraid someone had followed him. For a
while, we were all on pins and needles; no one
knew if he would out others on his way out the
door.

Although I was never called in, I talked to
OSI once, when I was undergoing a background
investigation for security clearance. I
recall one friend who was called into Security
Police investigations because his roommate
had reported him as being gay. Oddly enough,
that same roommate ended up making advances
toward me by blowing me kisses, but because he
had just turned in my friend, I ignored his
advances (although I was tempted). We used to
use little code words, like *Dandy*, to determine
who was safe to approach. If someone didn't

know who *Dandy* was, he didn't know what was going on; I wouldn't say anything to anyone who didn't know the code word. We never knew who was working undercover for OSI.

How was military life before Don't Ask, Don't Tell?

It did not take much to cause an investigation or get someone kicked out. When I was stationed in Abilene, Texas, a couple of gay airmen separated from the military, and afterwards they called back to tell the military who was gay. I kid around about what I would threaten to do to those men if they called and reported me, because I didn't want to get caught. They reported one guy just as he was about to leave on vacation; they called base security police, who stopped him at the gate before he could leave. Unfortunately, a search of his room turned up gay paraphernalia. Before Don't Ask, Don't Tell, it only took a rumor to get you kicked out!

How was life under Don't Ask, Don't Tell?

After Don't Ask, Don't Tell came around in 1992, I felt as though nothing had really changed. You could be gay, but you still couldn't participate in homosexual activities. I believe everyone in all branches of the military already knew who in their units was gay and who was not. When I was an E-3, my station chief from Jacksonville, North Carolina, said, "Yeah, I know gay people in the military. They are some of my best workers." And he looked at me. I thought, "That was noble."

More than anything, the fear surrounding gays serving openly in the military has to do with fearing the unknown. People do not know what to expect. They think openly gay military will turn the armed forces into a "pride parade." They fear what may happen in open-bay showers and so on; straight people fear they will be hit on. News flash: we have been among you for forever, and we do not want every man we see. More to the point, most of us know how to act in a professional setting.

How did you protect your career?

I do not remember anyone ever asking me if I was seeing someone. One of my biggest rules for dealing with people was that I *never* asked anyone anything about his personal life, and I expected the same treatment in return. The amazing thing is that a lot of the straight guys would flirt with me, usually after a couple of drinks. Now, the idea that all gay men have a voracious sexual appetite and will sleep with anyone is a fallacy. I never followed through on any of these guys' "innocent" flirtations. My goal was to have them say the same flirtatious things when they were sober. As you've probably guessed, I wouldn't hear from them again. Who knew if it was a set-up? People always knew where I stood, and everyone always loved me anyway. They accepted me for me.

I was also careful not to associate with overly flamboyant individuals—you know, the gay men that Stevie Wonder could pick out by looking at them. I also never gave out my work phone number to acquaintances, and I never had any of my romantic interests visit me at my place of work. All conversations related to any "gay" topic took place *only* in private locations.

I'll admit I did consider leaving the military. One of my brothers said he would get me a job at North Carolina State University, but I didn't have a degree. Lorenzo and I had a conversation about my future, discussing the fact that I didn't have a degree, that my car wasn't paid for, and that I didn't have money saved. So I decided to stay.

Did you come out to active-duty friends after retiring?

I still choose to keep my personal and public lives separate. My being the oldest of five may play a role in my reasoning. If someone asks me now, I will tell him; however, I have never reached out to tell anyone.

I believe that my straight friends get me. When I went back to Omaha, Nebraska, for a visit, everyone gave me a warm welcome and hugs. I am still very good friends with the Carters, a married couple I met while we were

in technical school for weather forecasting.
Mrs. Carter and I immediately bonded, and her
husband was never jealous of our relationship.
Sometimes we were stationed at the same base,
but no matter where Mrs. Carter and I were
stationed, we would always reach out to each
other; we could talk for hours. I intentionally
never told the Carters that I was gay. I didn't
want them to have to lie to anyone about what
they knew about me, whether the questions came
from a security clearance investigator or from
a coworker making casual conversation. The
Carters and I remain the best of friends to
this day. As a matter of fact, they stayed
with me during a recent hurricane on the East
Coast.

Would you serve again?

I believe that it would
be a good experience for
everyone to serve in the
military for at least
two years. I would do it
again because it made me
grow up, it allowed me
to see the world, and it
made me see myself and
others in a different
way. I learned how to
respect others and their
differences.

Interview with Brian E. Markowski (Ski)

I met Ski through Kenny, and Kenny met Ski while stationed in Germany. Kenny met Ski, and the result was a lifelong friendship. Because Kenny always talked about him, I felt like I knew Ski even before we met.

Kenny made Ski sound like someone I wanted to meet. In our world of keeping secrets, you needed friends you could trust, friends who were not self-destructive and apt to take you down with them. Ski is different from Kenny and me in that he did not stay in the military and retire. He did his time, separated from the military, and put down roots in Washington DC. This is something to be envied in the military, where the constant moving around does not allow you to settle into a community (although the last twelve years of my career gave me that rare opportunity). Ski is the glue that binds our group of friends together. He is "the hostess with the mostest," and people love to gather for his spirited functions. Since moving to the DC area, I have made new friends through my connection to Ski. Here is my interview with him.

Why did you join the military?

I grew up mainly in a single-parent home, with a father who was not there like he should have been. I watched my mother scrap and struggle for everything she had to provide for her family. I knew that attending college wasn't going to happen under the circumstances, because paying for college would have been so difficult. Even if my mother had been able to fund my college education, it would have been extremely hard on her. I decided to go into the military so that I could not only get an education but also become self-sufficient, which was my main goal.

Why did you choose the Air Force?

Out of my seven uncles, one was in the army, one was in the navy, and one went from being a marine into the army. I didn't want to follow any of those paths. The navy wasn't what I was looking for, but the Air Force offered options in the electronic field, which I was studying at the time; my technical high school had taught me electronics. My path was different from the ones all my uncles had taken, but I thought it was the ideal decision. It gave me a sense of being self-sufficient.

Tell me about your Military Entrance Processing Station experience.

During the application process, everyone was asked if he or she was gay. At the time,

I had been dating a woman for three years. When they asked me if I was gay, I said, "No, I'm not gay." At this point I was not aware of my true sexuality, so this was an honest answer. There were all kinds of medical tests, weight and height checks, and physical strength requirements. I followed their instruction closely and did what I was supposed to. Throughout the process, I felt that it was "their way or no way," and so I just told myself to do what I had to do. I had endured medical physicals before, but this one was quick, intimidating, and completely impersonal. I felt like a robot with a social security number—entirely without emotion.

During my final acceptance, I was sworn in by a marine. Although I was in the zone and not sexually active, I remember thinking that he had the body of a god. It was not a sexual thought; I simply saw this marine as the true essence of a military man. He had such confidence and presence, and his uniform was squared away. I aspired to be him.

Tell me about your basic training experience.

I felt guilty when I left for basic training because of my mother. My father was an alcoholic, and I was worried that he wouldn't be there for my mother when she needed help emotionally or financially. When I left she was at work, so I had to leave a note saying my goodbyes.

```
Mom and Dad,            June 8, 1989


I love you very much. Wish me luck.


Love,


Brian
```

It would be six days before I had a chance to speak with my parents again. Mom said she couldn't believe I left a note, and she was worried that I wasn't eating. What's funny is that my mother still has my note attached to my old bedroom closet door.

The reality of military life didn't hit me until about 2:00 a.m., as I approached my destination and started seeing guards and concrete buildings. At this point I began to question myself, asking what I had gotten myself into. I remember being hot and sweaty when I got off the bus, but my dorm rooms weren't ready yet. For two days I was in limbo, waiting for the rest of my flight members to arrive. Once they came, the fear took over.

The very first night with everyone there, the training instructors gave locks to us new arrivals and ordered us to open them without using any tools. I thought of my mom and what she would have said: "You'd just better get it done." I was the first one to open my lock, cutting my finger in the process. I raised my hand and told the TI, who allowed me to get a tissue and take care of the cut.

At that point I was still the same person, but I was on edge, functioning at a different level. It helped that everyone else was there, because I knew I wasn't completely alone. I'll admit that I cried like a baby when I called my mom for the first time. We talked about basic training and how I wasn't getting much sleep; I would be up half the night second-guessing myself, wondering if I had read what I should have or if I had properly memorized the Air Force history.

Tell me about your drill instructors.

I have a vivid memory of the "snake pit," where all the training instructors would sit together and eat during mealtimes. One time in particular I was walking past the snake pit and a TI called out to "Airman Markowitz."

Since that wasn't my name, I didn't answer and just kept on walking. A few moments after I sat down, I felt the TI come up behind me. I could feel his eyes on me, his breath and everything, as he leaned down to speak into my left ear. "Boy," he said, "you hear me talking to you?"

"No, sir," I said, explaining that I did not answer because he had pronounced my last name incorrectly. He understood and moved along. Although he didn't say my name correctly, I had respectfully stated my reason for ignoring him. From that time on, I was called "Pretty Boy Ski"—or just "Ski" because it was easier to pronounce.

Another memorable moment from basic training was when I was pulling night guard duty and one of the TIs specifically told me not to let anyone in after 9:00 p.m. Later, that same TI came up and knocked on door, but it was after 9:00 p.m., so I did what I had been instructed to do. I asked the TI to prove his authority, but he didn't have his badge or uniform on, so I refused entry. The TI had clearly said not to let anyone in, and I didn't. I spent the whole shift on edge, wondering if he was going to come back.

The next morning I was standing at attention in line, ready to start my day, when I heard the taps of my instructor's shoes. All I could feel was dread; I knew I was dead in the water. He approached from behind, leaned forward, and whispered into my ear, "Good job."

The TIs had a little fun at our expense during mail call. My TI would embarrass me in front of everyone. At the time, I had a girlfriend who sent me perfume-scented letters. Whenever one arrived, the TI would toss it to me, saying, "Here's your damn perfume envelope."

At the end of graduation from basic training, after we marched and gave a salute to the base commander, our TI said, "Good job, airmen." I felt that I had finally made it, and it was with the help of my TI that I got there. He was tough, but he did what he had to do, and he also had a heart. Everyone was terrified of him, though, which helped perpetuate his tough reputation.

Not everyone completed basic training. Some people quit, some had a nervous breakdown, and a few even tried to kill themselves. Basic training was tough!

Tell me about your first duty station.

My first assignment was to Ramstein Air Base in Germany. I originally had orders for Bergstrom Air Force Base in Austin, but I did not want to stay in Texas; I wanted to see the world. One of my flight members asked if I wanted to switch orders, which is how I ended up in Germany.

I got to Germany on New Year's Eve, after a fourteen-hour-long flight. On the flight with me was an attractive young lady with green eyes who reminded me of my girlfriend at the time. While she was very pretty, she was also very quiet and kept to herself. I didn't know it then, but we would become friends. I arrived on base not really knowing what to do next. Once I got to my dorm room, the situation started to hit me: I was far from home, it was New Year's Eve, and I didn't even know what time it was.

I had a third-floor room, and there were two people to each dorm. My room was vacant, so I was lucky enough to have the room to myself for the next two months. At the time I worked in flight operations, and one day when I came home from work, I noticed someone else's bags in my room—my roommate had arrived. The adjustment was something I had to get accustomed to; I simply had to deal with the lack of privacy and everything else that comes with having a roommate.

Dr. Lorenzo L. McFarland with Brian E. Markowski, T. David Gilmer, and
Kenneth N. Brooks

What did you learn from your first supervisor?

My first supervisor always said to "follow through"—one of those things you learn in basic training. Sometimes that meant checking on coworkers to ensure they did what *they* were supposed to do. When inspection time came, regardless of what you did right, you could still get into trouble because others did not follow through. My sergeant had gotten into trouble for things that didn't get done, so she always told everyone to "follow through," and it stuck with me.

I will never forget being at Ramstein when a C5 cargo plane crashed at Frankfurt Air Base. Ramstein was the closest base to the crash site, so everyone on my flight line had to help with the cleanup. Riding up to the crash site, I saw the bodies of Air Force personnel, some still strapped into their seats. This was something I had never seen before, and it was disturbing. I did not want to help with the cleanup. But at the end of the day I felt a lot better because I had helped my fellow military members in some way. We brought back the wreckage and secured the area so that investigators could determine that cause of the crash and perhaps prevent such a thing from happening in the future—and it was all because I followed through. About a month after the crash, the family members of those who died went to the flight line and listened to me and others talk about the crash. I felt I was supporting my family, my military family.

Tell me about military women.

I met a woman named Alison in Germany, while I was modeling for one of the local stores. Alison was also a model, so I saw her all the time. Although she was married, she still pursued me. It started when she asked if I was going to an upcoming fashion show, and the next thing I knew she was pushing me to hang out other places. Three or four months later, the night of the fashion show, we had sex, and afterwards she wouldn't leave me alone. It was getting really messy. I was jeopardizing my career because she happened to be married to another military member. She also worked at the base federal credit union, which meant I had to see her when I needed money. I began finding reasons to avoid her, and finally she started dating another military airman, which let me off the hook. I liked her, but I knew the situation was not right. I had let myself get into this situation because of my breakup with my fiancé. It didn't help that she looked like my ex.

Tell me about your first time going to a gay bar while in the military.

When I first got to Germany, I was engaged to my girlfriend from back home. Six months after arriving in Germany, she came for a visit. I wanted to officially propose when I saw her, so I saved my money and bought a ring, only to find out she had come with three of her best friends. I was a bit frustrated. I had made arrangements with my roommate for her to stay in the dorms with me, but that was out the window, and now I had to find housing for her friends. I never got the chance to propose, and I knew something wasn't right because she was acting very differently than she had six months before. I starting asking her friends what was wrong with her, but they said she was just nervous and not sure how to react to seeing me.

I had planned a day trip to Paris to propose; I was going to ask her at the Eiffel Tower to marry me. I will never forget that she wore a black-and-white polka-dotted dress. While we were taking a boat ride, I finally asked if she would marry me—and she said no, because she was dating someone else. Confused and mad, I left her when we got back to the port. I walked back to our room, packed up my things, and moved to another hotel. Both of us were upset, but we never really got a chance to talk about it.

When she returned back to the States, I struggled to understand what had happened. For consolation I started talking to my friend Blanca, who lived near me, and over time I became very fond of her. We starting hanging out, going to eat, and so on. As our friendship grew, I noticed that she had a mysterious life and seemed to keep secrets from me. For example, she lived in off-base housing, and when I visited her there, I had to call beforehand. I didn't know why, and I also wondered why I hadn't met all her friends.

One night Blanca and her friends invited me to a German nightclub. I happily went, thinking Blanca and I were going on a date. There were guys kissing guys and girls kissing girls, but this wasn't different from other German clubs I had seen, so I didn't think much of it. Then I went to the bathroom and noticed two sets of feet in one of the stalls. I peeked under and couldn't see anything, but I knew something wasn't right. I came back out and said to my friends, "People are making out in the stall—watch when they come out." I thought it was going to be two girls, but when two guys came out instead, I was very surprised. I said to Blanca, "Two guys just came out of the bathroom!" and Blanca said, "Yeah, this is a gay club." I immediately walked out, because I was scared of being seen in a gay club when I was in the military. My friends came out to check on me, but I felt betrayed and upset. They confessed that they were gay and they thought I was, too. I left to go back to base.

A few days later, my friends came around and explained more things about the military and being gay. It turned out that Blanca had a female partner who was also in the military. I admired their relationship and came to understand why Blanca had been so secretive. I began to accept what my friends told me, and I still wanted to be their friend. However, I still didn't know whether I was gay. I was at Club Nanou one night when a man named Larry, also in the military, told Blanca that he liked me. I had seen him around and thought he was interesting, but I wasn't sure if his interest was in friendship or more. Blanca told me that Larry just wanted to hang out with me and be friends—and I needed a friend, considering what I had just gone through with my ex fiancé. So Larry and I started hanging out, going to the gym, and doing other things. One night, when we were drinking at the club, we kissed. I was scared, but it felt good.

Still, Larry wanted it, but I didn't. I had become very fond of Larry, and we were good friends, but I still wasn't sure if I was gay. We started hanging out more and more, I would visit Larry at his place, and eventually we had a sexual encounter. I just remember being intoxicated and the next morning thinking, "What the hell did I do?" Larry was very reassuring; he understood that I was conflicted about the situation. I went home and told Blanca and the gang what happened.

Over the next three months, Larry and I talked over the situation and explored my sexuality. I was still talking to other girls on the base, and Larry knew about my straight life, which caused some conflict. I finally made a decision and started a relationship with Larry. I thought Larry was a bit too obviously gay, so I limited our interactions to the post office and gym; when we ran into each other on base, we acted like strangers. Larry lived off base, which provided some privacy.

Tell me about your experience with HIV/AIDS in the military.

When I was getting ready to leave Germany, Larry called from the states to tell me that he was HIV-positive. My first thought was "No way"—but then I immediately went out and got tested. My results came back negative, but everything started setting in when I thought about Larry and how he hadn't been safe. I felt angry, upset, and sad, but I decided that I still had to be his friend; after all, he was the first gay man I had ever been with. I also wondered if Larry had to tell the military whom he had been with. I was scared even to talk about it on my own telephone. I felt anger and anguish—and I felt selfish, because I was thinking of myself and not Larry.

I had to lie when I went to the military clinic to get tested. I said that my partner had been diagnosed with HIV, pretending it was a female partner. Back then, being gay was an extreme taboo and would have ended my military career. I felt isolated and thought about all the things I might never get to do. If my results were positive, what would I do? I had used protection, but that is never a sure thing.

I was relieved to learn that I was healthy, but I also felt worse because Larry had to go through his illness alone. This was a very lonely time period for me. All my military friends were stationed elsewhere, and this was before e-mail and Facebook. I was overseas, and the only available mode of communication was the telephone, which I didn't dare use on a military base. I survived, but it would have been nice to have a friend by my side.

Later, another very close friend in the military notified me that he was HIV-positive. My first reaction was, "What about your career?" I wondered how he had let this happen. He was part of my military family—we were like brothers. I had so many questions: "What are other people going to think?" "Should I tell our friends?" "What are you going to do?" I was both angry and sad, seeing what my friend had to go through. He told me about all the medical test and examinations, saying he felt like a "lab rat." This was in 1994, before the triple therapy treatment, when they were still losing a lot of people to HIV/AIDS.

After eighteen years of service, my friend decided to leave with an honorable discharge, leaving his retirement behind in the process. He now lives in Washington DC, and we are still friends.

Any experiences with the Office of Special Investigations?

To my knowledge, I was never investigated by OSI, but I was questioned about someone else's sexuality. I had already known that a "witch hunt" was going on—this was our code word meaning that an OSI investigation was happening and they were trying to find gays in the military. When word got out, everyone would stay out of the clubs and wouldn't even interact with one another, just to make sure they wouldn't be exposed. One day I heard a knock on my dorm door—it was a female OSI agent. I played dumb as she asked about my friend Blanca. Often a witch hunt would be focused on one person, but the investigation would turn up the names of other people, which then led to the OSI questioning them. The OSI would ask questions without telling you exactly what they were investigating.

Blanca survived the witch hunt, but it turns out that her best girlfriend was being investigated—that's how Blanca got on the OSI's radar. I wasn't sure if my name ever came up. My friends were petrified; they didn't want to eat out, get their nails done, go to the gym, or do anything public, because they didn't know who might be looking over their shoulders.

It's kind of funny that some of the most obviously gay people escaped detection. One male airman on the base would go to the gay club wearing ripped-up military uniforms, high-heeled shoes, and a bandana on his head, and I remember saying to myself, "He seems like a lot of fun—but how do I know he isn't really OSI?" This guy was really overboard, so I wasn't sure. I would be nice to him, say hi, and buy him an occasional drink, but that was it. We had strict rules that we followed when we went out to the gay clubs. First, we would always arrive and leave together. If one of us met someone while we were out, we all had to go to the person's house together or back to the base together. Although we would take our military IDs into the clubs, we would park blocks away.

How was military life before Don't Ask, Don't Tell?

Being gay in the military was just part of my lifestyle. I didn't know what the military would do if they found out I was gay; I felt like a second-class citizen. Back in 1990, a man on my flight line simply didn't show up to work one day, and everyone wondered where he went. Next thing we knew, he had been kicked out because he was gay. I wondered what they did to him. Where did he go? Was he in prison?

How was military life under Don't Ask, Don't Tell?

Life in the military did not change because of DADT; I still had boundaries under which I

served. I felt that the real fear of gays comes
from the unknown, from people worrying that
everyone in the military would become gay if
we were allowed to serve openly. I also think
some straight people are afraid they might act
on something they don't want to act on—there
are a lot of closeted people in the military.

How did you protect your career?

I never knew what someone was going to ask
me, so I always had to be prepared to answer
questions about my sexuality. Once, after I
visited a friend living off base in Germany, a
guard at the gate who knew me asked me where
I was coming from. It was 6:30 a.m.; I had
to think of something quickly. So I lied and
said I had been visiting my godchild's house
and had spent the night. Normally that guard
worked one certain gate, so another time I
purposely went around to the other side of the
base to avoid her. I was using my friend's car,
and she recognized it. Again I had to make up
a lie, saying something was wrong with my car
so I used my friend's to go see my godchild.
You always have to be quick, ready to deflect
a question at a moment's notice. This girl
watched me too closely and I needed to get her
off my back. Maybe I was letting my suspicions
get the best of me, but it was always better
to be safe than sorry.

Why did you leave the military?

My separation from the military didn't have
anything to do with my being gay. I was simply

tired of moving every six or seven months; I felt like I couldn't ever focus on anything, including relationships. I got very tired of the lifestyle. So although a factor in my leaving was my sexuality, it wasn't the primary factor. Once I separated from the military, I felt better. I didn't have to look over my shoulder—but I still did, from time to time. Old habits die hard.

My partner, David, knew I had served in the military, but when we met he did not mention that he was currently in the military, working at the Pentagon. I understand. He had to protect his career; it was a big secret to entrust to anyone. When David was still on active duty, I wanted to attend military functions with him, but, as you know, that was impossible. Even now, people at David's work do not know a lot about him.

Did you come out to active-duty friends after separating?

About six or seven years ago, one of my good friends started e-mailing me and asked if I was married yet. I decided to just tell her no, that I was gay and had a partner. I also said in the e-mail that I hoped that fact wouldn't change our relationship. Within twenty minutes she called and said that she had thought I was gay but felt it wasn't her place to ask—and that she loved me as a person, so it didn't matter. I felt bad for not having told her during all those years we served together; I was just conditioned that way from the military. I still don't volunteer much information, just in case. I don't want to jeopardize things. Currently, I have pictures of David on my desk. I do not tell people who he is, but if asked, I tell the truth.

Would you serve again?

I would do it all again, because it had such a monumental impact on life. It made me a man. It exposed me to different cultures and expanded my mind. Although my coworkers and I came from different walks of life, we had the same mission, which was to defend the United States. If not for the military, I would not be where I am today, and I wouldn't have met most of my closest friends.

If given the chance to openly serve, I wouldn't. I would keep it the same because my sexuality doesn't identify me. I am a man, and my being gay is just a part of the entire package. Although I would like to say yes to the question about serving openly, I can't. While it would have been nice not to feel that someone was out to get me, if I hadn't served when I did, I might not have become who I am today. I like who I am—and some of it is due to having served in silence. That made me strong!

Interview with T. David Gilmer

David Gilmer is the newest member of this group of military friends. I was introduced to David through Ski. It should be noted that David and Ski are partners; 2011 marked their fifth anniversary. I love David because he makes Ski happy. They portray a part of the gay community that many people believe doesn't exist—a committed gay couple. During a party to celebrate their anniversary, David shared a beautiful story of his daily life with Ski: every day, Ski packs David's lunch and leaves him a handwritten note. Gay or straight, this is the sort of life we would all like to share with someone.

I value the fact that David brings a different element to this group, having been married to a woman and fathered two children. And while most of the comments in this book reflect experiences from the Air Force, David provides a refreshing perspective of life as a gay man in the navy.

Why did you join the military?

I was looking for a way out of my small town in southern Indiana, so I signed up for the navy when I was seventeen, through the Delayed Entry Program. Two months after graduating from high school, I was off to boot camp. The simple truth is I chose the navy because of the cool advertisements. Plus the recruiter really hyped up the lifestyle, as if it were just being out to sea and seeing the world from one port to the next. Needless to say, I was ready to leave Indiana and travel the world.

Tell me about your basic training experience.

I went to basic training in Orlando, Florida. I was sad to leave home, never having been away from my mother, brother, and sisters. Hell, I had never even left my small town in southern Indiana. I often wondered if I had made the right decision in joining the navy. Growing up as the youngest of four, I always felt one step behind. I wasn't the smartest or the quickest, and from time to time my parents

would put me down. After high school graduation, I couldn't leave home fast enough. I wanted to prove my parents wrong, and being on my own was my first chance to do it.

The first seventy-two hours of basic training were bittersweet. My first call home was to my mother, and I cried like a baby—just like everyone else. This made me feel better, or at least like I was in the same boat as the others.

During basic training my nickname was "Slide-By-Boot-Camp Gilmer" because I never got into trouble; I just flew under the radar. Basic training was dramatic, being surrounded by different cultures and different people. I wasn't sure how to take it. And I had never shared space with so many people—twenty—to thirty-man units sleeping in the same area, showering together, etc.

We had an open-bay shower in our dorm, and I struggled to keep my head down and not check out guys. I forced myself not to look. I guess even then I was struggling with my sexuality. Having a gay older brother put me in a position where I felt obligated to carry on the family name. Thinking back on the shower scene, I realize I wasn't the only one struggling not to check out my neighbor.

Tell me about your drill instructors.

I had two old-school instructors, the epitome of old navy chiefs. They did not try to make you feel warm; they did their jobs and did not get personal with you. I was the quiet one, so they offered me the job of administrative assistant, but I declined. Administrative assistants were thought of as feminine or gay, and I didn't want to be associated with that stereotype. I felt that I had to be the masculine one in the family.

A bittersweet experience was my selection to the rifle team. I was supposed to march with the team during graduation, but two days before the ceremony, the drill instructors noticed that I did not have the strength to get my rifle high enough in the air. They withdrew me from the rifle march and put me back with my original company. I felt like a failure, but I got over it!

Tell me about your first duty station.

My first duty station was in Long Beach, California. I recall walking to my first ship with my mentor—I had this enormous sea bag, and I felt overwhelmed because it was such a handful. When I made it on board, my sea bag was tossed down a steep ladder well, and when I made it to my room, I found I had ten roommates sharing a very confined space. This, I realized, would be home for the next three years.

My first impression was that the living space was way too small and the people were a bit rude. The racks (beds) were mounted three high, looking a little like coffins on top of each other, and I had to lift up the mattress just to get to my locker/dresser. Everything had to be placed or rolled up in a certain way—there was no room for error. A little blue curtain gave you some privacy in the rack.

I had to deal with sailors snoring and people with poor hygiene. Also, the commodes would frequently overflow, completely covering the floor with waste and water. Things like this happen on a ship; some things work properly, and some things did not from time to time. I woke up too many mornings with crap on the floor—that was ship life, and at times it was awful. It was a huge adjustment, and it really made me appreciate my life off the ship.

I was told that sailors had to share racks.

Top racking is where sleeping space is shared by more than one person. If somebody works nights, they relinquish their personal space to their shipmate who works days. This is practiced only on submarines.

What did you learn from your first supervisor?

I learned a lot about navy traditions, because my first supervisor was all about showing the new guys those traditions, especially the things they'd put the younger sailors through. I remember them being somewhat tortuous, such as "pink bellies." Pink Bellies are a tradition used by enlisted sailors to welcome newly arrived members into their berthing (sleeping quarters onboard ship). Usually a party of four would hold the new sailor down on a table or the floor. The prank includes pouring water on the stomach and slapping it until it turns pink. They also liked to put the new sailors in awkward situations. For example, they would have a "metal buoy watch," which meant a sailor had to go in front of the pointy part of the ship, near the head gear, and try to wave down the mail helicopter. I recall doing this and being completely humiliated. Half the people aboard the ship would be watching you out there waving your flags; meanwhile, the ship would be moving up and down, and you had to try and keep your balance. Then they would tell you, "Well, the helicopter is going to the back of the ship," so you had to run to catch it, but there would be guys hiding behind doors with buckets of ice-cold water, and as you ran past they would splash you, saying, "Watch out for the waves!" My supervisor was the mastermind behind it all.

So what did you learn?

I learned to watch my back, pay attention to details, work hard, and follow directions.

How did you handle discovering your true sexuality?

I met my wife while transferring from my first duty station. I was at the mall, and I had a little competition with a friend to see who could get the most phone numbers from females. I met Felicia during this little competition. When I got home, I pulled out the phone numbers I had collected and decided to call her. The following day we went to Venice Beach for our first date. We started dating, one thing led to another, and six months later, Felicia was pregnant. We married after our son Ricco was born.

When my brother came out of the closet at seventeen, I felt I had to be the one to have a traditional family and give my parents grandchildren. At the time, a gay lifestyle wasn't part of my daily life; I had never even thought about it. When I was younger, however, I had questions. I was molested by one of my brother's boyfriends—it happened more than once, though I didn't say or do anything about it—and I wondered if that would trigger gay feelings in me down the road. But when I met

Felicia, we lived a traditional lifestyle. We moved to San Diego and built a life from there.

In 1993, my brother passed away from HIV, which he contracted from his partner. My mother told people that my brother died of a blood transfusion; she didn't know how to explain the truth to people. So that became the party line for the family: for years I told people in the navy that my brother had died of a blood transfusion. At the time, my son wasn't even a year old, and I started going to counseling in the gay community. It took my brother's death for me to deal with my sexuality and break down some of the walls that I had constructed around me.

I felt very comfortable at the counseling center and started hanging out with gay men without Felicia and Ricco. I found an emotional bond with my new friends. My feeling of comfort in the gay community made me question my sexuality, but at the same time, I knew I was in a loving relationship. My second son, Miles, came along a year and half later.

I continued to hang out with my gay friends, going to nightclubs as a guest. Sometimes Felicia would go with me to gay clubs, and she would become very defensive when a man showed interest in me. I wasn't looking for a relationship, though—just having fun with my friends. I started to feel like I could let my guard down and talk about anything with my gay friends, and that's when my transition started. With my wife, children, and other family members, I felt artificial. Felicia would question me about things I did, like getting haircuts and going out to gay clubs, but I wasn't doing anything behind her back.

She questioned the haircuts, because I changed my hair style. I think it was too much change for her. I was simply bored with straight men talking about sports and women. I didn't connect with them. With my friends in the gay community, I felt connected and alive.

It was as if I had a split personality. I felt comfortable with my family, but I also enjoyed the new life that I was discovering. Still, I knew I shouldn't go down that road. I didn't want to disappoint my mother and my family, and I felt conflicted about my life in the gay scene. I would meet some wonderful people who showed interest in me, but I couldn't engage. On one occasion, I met an older guy and found that I had feelings for him; we would sit for hours and talk and just be in the moment. I remember crying because I could not be with this man.

Felicia was very suspicious and would question me about my new friends. And I held on for as long as I could. I didn't want to leave while my children were young. Eventually, however, the stress between my wife and me was too much to handle. I'll have to admit that the urge to be with men was also a contributing factor.

What was it like having women serve on a ship?

When I first entered the military, the navy allowed only men to serve on ships. The transition to women serving on ships was difficult for everyone. Some men found it hard to accept because they had to change their day-to-day activities. Now, for example, they couldn't just walk around in their boxers.

Men and women were always hooking up on the ship. I recall one group of women who thought they could take you away from whatever you had—your wife, your kids, and your girlfriend. I had to put up a thick skin so they wouldn't even think about approaching me in that way. I made it a point to talk a lot about Felicia and the boys.

Tell me about your first visit to a gay bar while in the military.

I joined the navy in 1989 and was there until 1992. My friends were all African-American men, and they were all about the girls and hanging out at straight clubs. Then one day I was invited to a party by a guy on the ship who was different from my usual group of friends. He had a Goth kind of style, with the black eyeliner and black clothes. When my friends spotted me talking with the "weird guy," they warned me not to hang out with him. I could tell he was disappointed.

When I joined the navy I didn't know anything about going to gay clubs or even that I was gay. My first duty station was all about hanging out with the guys, having fun, and doing what my straight friends were doing. It wasn't until my second duty station, when my brother passed away, that I started meeting a lot of gay men. My trip into the gay community for counseling eventually led me to my lifestyle change.

Tell me about your experience with HIV/

Dr. Lorenzo L. McFarland with Brian E. Markowski, T. David Gilmer, and Kenneth N. Brooks

AIDS while in the military.

During my counseling sessions to cope with the loss of my brother, I met a guy named John. I learned that John was in the navy and that we were stationed at the same base. Once I actually saw him on base, and we shared stories about why we were attending counseling. John said he was HIV-positive, which was why he was going for help. He was a culinary specialist and was no longer able to work in that area because of his diagnosis. I connected with John because of my brother's passing, so although I wasn't able to be there for my brother's illness, I was able to see what he had endured through my friendship with John.

I never really feared having an HIV test, but the navy did not do a good job protecting the privacy of people with HIV. At the navy station in San Diego, California, people with HIV were housed together in a particular dorm; if you lived there, everyone on base knew that you were HIV-positive—they might as well have put a large letter *A* on your chest.

I always used protection when having sex, but there was one occasion that freaked me out. I had sex with a guy, and afterwards he said, "Oh, I forgot to tell you that I'm HIV-positive," as if it were the most natural thing in the world to say. He explained that people would brush him off when he would tell them up front. I was pissed. I know that being safe means you have to treat everyone as if he might have something, but it's still my right to choose whether to have sex with someone who actually does.

Any experience with Navy Crime Investigation Services?

There were some clear rules to follow if you did not want to become the focus of an NCIS investigation: If you go to a gay club, never pull out your military identification card. And if someone asks you if you are in the military, say no. That's because NCIS would plant good-looking girls and guys to hang out at the clubs to entrap younger, inexperienced gays. I used to go out all the time by myself, and I had my own rules, like never taking my military identification to the club. I also put a sticker over the military decal on my car so that no one would know I was in the navy.

How did you protect your career?

I put a lot of lies out there to protect both my career and lifestyle, so I had to make sure to keep track of the lies I told. Remembering things I had said about where I'd gone and whom I had been with was all part of the cover. My ex-wife, who knew I was gay, constantly threatened me if I didn't do what she said. I was past the ten-year mark with the navy; retirement was right down the road. I had to support my kids, and I was scared to death because I didn't want to lose my career and family.

It's still hard to talk about my lifestyle today. Even after having retired from the navy, I'm careful about sharing my sexuality. Recently I went to lunch with a coworker who wanted to get to know more about me as a friend. After I told him I was gay, he said he had figured as much, but he felt it wasn't his place to ask. I generally can point out which of my coworkers would be okay with my sexuality.

Would you serve again?

I would serve again! I know a lot of people from my hometown who are still stuck in the same place. The military provided me opportunities I never would have had at home and enabled me to learn things I wouldn't have learned otherwise. Basic training alone takes you out of your comfort zone; sleeping next to all sorts of different people, you get used to having others around you.

If I were given the chance to openly serve, I would not. When you already have things going against you, such as your race or where you are from, being openly gay would make military life that much harder. I also believe that past a certain point in the military, it's all about politics. If you are known to be gay and the promotion board doesn't like it, you won't excel.

Coming Out to Active-Duty and Military Friends

By Dr. Lorenzo McFarland

While I was writing this book, it struck me that including insights from some of my former coworkers might provide a different and helpful perspective. It was a great idea but a frightening one, too. After all these years, I still find it hard to tell people that I am gay—the fear of rejection is powerful. My current relationships might not be perfect, but at least I have them. Coming out may cost me a friend or two. Well, I thought, I can deal with it now or deal with it when the book comes out.

In the past, when I moved or when a coworker moved, it meant the end of our relationship, although there were a few friends with whom I crossed paths again. I chose to let go of a lot of my friendships with straight people in the military because I couldn't be me around them. Usually I would have preferred to keep them as friends, but over time they started to ask too many questions.

Facebook was a game-changer. Through Facebook I have reconnected with people I knew in the first grade. The same goes for my former military coworkers; we are connected in a way that would not have been possible ten years ago. This is potentially problematic, because I do not remember what lies I told to keep my secret. Now that I am out, more people from my past will know it. So I reached out to previous coworkers, telling them about the book and stating for a fact that I am gay.

In the past, the process of reaching out to people would have required writing a letter or e-mail or placing a phone call. Today I communicate with my friends through Facebook. I do not spend a lot of time on Facebook, but it's great for announcing or acknowledging birthdays, wedding, births, moves, and promotions. I have some friends who post several times a day, but most of my friends only share major life events. In preparation for the publication of this book, I reached out to ten former coworkers using the following Facebook message:

I hope all is well with you. I'm having a blast in DC working for the Veterans Health Administration in the Office of Public Health. I'm directly involved with policy, planning, and guidance for Hepatitis C, HIV/AIDS, and tobacco. I am also writing to tell you about another one of my initiatives. Not sure if you ever thought about my sexuality, but I am gay. I'm telling you now because I'm in the process of writing a book with several friends on Don't Ask, Don't Tell and what it's like to be gay and serve in the military. It's a work in progress, but I wanted to share with you.

Lorenzo

I sent the message out on a Saturday night—which, in hindsight, was a bad idea. I had a hard time sleeping with my mind racing over the possible responses I would get back. I have pretty good taste in friends, so my first thoughts were positive; I felt that I had friendships that were not based on sexuality or even political agendas. But the reality is that the military changes people, and with the recent decision to repeal Don't Ask, Don't Tell, I had no idea how my old friends would receive my news. Change is hard, and this change was no different than the integration of blacks and women into the military.

The first response I received was from my last military adoptive mother, DeeDee Millican. Let me explain that throughout my military career, I had four adoptive mothers. I may have been thousands of miles from home, but I always had someone special to watch over me. DeeDee was my last adoptive mother while I was stationed at Brooks City-Base in San Antonio. Her response was immediate:

> Lorenzo
>
> I don't care what your sexuality is -- you are my precious adopted son and I love you. You and Spence are very special to me and always will be. I am so proud of you . . . looking forward to reading your book.
>
> Love ya Mom

Her e-mail made me smile and reassured me that our relationship was one of mutual admiration. I was hopeful that the rest of my friends would feel the same way.

The second response came from a friend I have known since the summer of 1987. Captain Shelia Grady and I met during technical training school. She was a little ball of fire, and several guys wanted to hook up with her, but she stood her ground. Over the years we would meet up at various military functions. In 1995, I accepted an assignment to the United States School of Aerospace Medicine as an Air Force instructor. Shelia was already stationed at Brooks Air Force Base, working for the school's consultation services. We reconnected, and a year or so later I helped her move into an instructor position. We forged a strong relationship, both on and off duty. As strong as that relationship was, however, I never felt comfortable disclosing my sexuality to her. I wasn't surprised by her response to my message, but I was relieved.

Lorenzo,

Hey there. Thanks for sharing your status with me. I've also suspected but it never really mattered other than I was a little sad you couldn't be yourself around me. I want you to know I love you for you. As for the book, you already have two buyers . . . me and Paul and my parents. Mom and Dad said to say hello.

Shelia

Shelia is such a sweet person, and she has a story that other young women could learn from.

I have always admired her courage and strong parenting skills. Her values kept her girls grounded and gave them a great work ethic. Because I admire her, I really wanted to hear her perspective on our friendship and the idea of gays serving openly in the military. Since she showed keen interest in the book I thought it would be great if she contributed her point of view.

Shelia,

I knew you knew, but it's always better when it's out in the open. I almost told you back in 1998 but just couldn't get it out. It's a hard thing to say, especially when I had done physicals of several of my friends who were being administratively separated. You actually hit on one of the topics for my book. You, Claudio, and my first supervisor, to name a few, are people that I would have wanted to tell about my sexuality. It was frustrating not being able to tell you guys. I felt cheated in not having a complete friendship. I could never bring a date to any of the functions or even just talk about my love life. I want to have different perspectives in my book, especially from my friends. If you would like to be included, I would love to have a short essay or story from your viewpoint on our relationship, how we interacted at work and off duty, and whether you think it would have made a difference if I could have been openly gay. Also, let me know if you want your name mentioned or not. I want to give credit if you want it, but I also want to respect your privacy. Let me know if you are interested.

Lorenzo

She happily agreed:

```
Lorenzo,

You are so awesome. I wish you would have told me,
but I totally get why you felt like you couldn't.
I'd love to contribute to your book. As a matter of
fact, I too am thinking of writing a book. My vision
is to help women with low self-esteem, using myself
as a basis and how my low self-esteem contributed
to my many dysfunctional relationships. Now that
I know my own self-worth, I would love to help
others break the cycle. Anyway, I'll start working
on a short story you can use. I already have it in
my head, just need to write it down. Oh before I
forget and now that we can talk about it, do you
have a special someone in your life? I hope so. No
one deserves it more than you.

Shelia
```

By Captain Shelia Grady

As I look back on my military career and all
the friendships I've developed none stand out
more than my friendship with Lorenzo McFarland.
We became friends in the summer of 1987 and have
remained friends ever since. Lorenzo, I'd have
to say is more like a brother to me. Since our
friendship began, he and I have gone through
challenging moments in both our careers and
our personal lives. I've sought his counsel on
more than one occasion. I remember one occasion
when I was feeling particularly insecure about
myself and I turned to Lorenzo and asked him
if I was ugly because I couldn't get a date. He
very sweetly told me I was beautiful and that
sometimes guys can be intimidated by that.
Great answer right? He always had the right

words. He was a rock I could always lean on. I had hoped that I had provided him with the same sense of dependability but now know that his ability to share with me was limited.

In May 2011, Lorenzo relayed his sexual orientation to me and others he considers friends. Although I've always suspected, I never asked him if he was gay. Mainly because the answer wouldn't change the way I felt about him. He was and is my friend who I love unconditionally. The other reason I never asked was because of the military's stance on homosexuality. If I had asked Lorenzo and he had told me the truth, I would no longer have plausible deniability and he'd have to wonder if I told anyone else.

Looking back, I have to wonder how he managed it all. Keeping secrets isn't easy, especially one that is so fundamental to whom you are as a person. Lorenzo and I worked together as

instructors teaching emergency medicine. The
cadre of instructors we worked with were our
friends too. We would often hang out together
during our off duty hours. We had a great time
together hang-out with our families. Many of
us would bring our children, spouses, or even
a date to social events. Lorenzo would always
bring his mother, Odell, never a date. I wonder
if I could have managed living with constraints
like the ones Lorenzo lived with. Not sharing
the intimate details of a relationship is one
thing but not being able to even say I'm in a
relationship is altogether something different,
especially when you are surrounded by others
who are able to freely share their status.

As a member of the Armed Forces, I'll admit
that I had my reservations about the repeal of
Don't Ask Don't Tell. Having been in the Air
Force since 1987 and deployed several times, I
wasn't sure how we as a military set in tradition
would manage the change. Personally, I wouldn't
want to share a room with a lesbian. Not because
I'm fearful or don't like gay women but for
the same reasons I wouldn't want to share a
room with a man. Although he or she may not be
attracted to me, they are attracted to certain
body parts that aren't always easy to hide in
a deployed environment. The situation would be
uncomfortable for me and them which isn't fair
to either of us. That being said, I support the
President and his decision to repeal the act.
Not just because he is my Commander In Chief,
although that reason is more than sufficient,
but because it is the right thing to do. You
see out of all the people I have worked with,
none of them worked hard than Lorenzo. He was
a great instructor and was highly praised by
the faculty we worked with and students we

taught. His methods for training were creative, fun, and most importantly effective. I believe strongly that if he had experienced the same sense of freedom I had he would have been even better. How can one truly realize their full potential when they have to use so much of their energy hiding the truth about themselves? No one should have to hide who they are to serve their country.

Lorenzo,

Just read your write up and it's beautiful. It brought a tear to my eye. You are such a beautiful person and I am so blessed to be able to call you friend. Love you!

Shelia

Next, I reached out to my first supervisor at the USAF School of Aerospace Medicine. I'll admit that I thought she hated me when I first started working for her; however, I came to understand that she had a very high standard for black men. Because there are so many negative stereotypes about black men, we have to perform above expectations just to be seen in the same light as our white counterparts. I get it, and I thank her for pushing me to be better.

```
Lorenzo,

Wow . . . great on your work, and you are correct,
sometimes we wondered whether you were or not. But
at the end of the day you did your job in an AWESOME
fashion, and for me that was enough.

Sharon
```

Feeling pretty good about reconnecting with friends and coming out to them, I reached out to another fellow instructor, Claudio Castillo—now *Chief* Castillo. It's amazing how far we have all come. During those early years as instructors, we were all struggling staff sergeants, dreaming of the day we would be at the top of our profession. It would be nice to be working with Chief Castillo, possibly discussing career field issues with him and helping him guide this new generation. I bailed on the dream, however—not so much for greener pastures, just other pastures.

```
Lorenzo,

Rebecca and I have always known, but it has never
mattered to us because you have always been a brother
to us. It is people with narrow minds that it matters
to. I am and have always been proud to serve with you!
We love you!

Claudio
```

The next response I received was from a former coworker at Minot Air Force Base. I was the manager of the Physical Examinations and Standards Section, and Richard was my second in command. We had a good group of airmen working for us, but many of them were unhappy. Minot was a tough place to be for your first Air Force assignment, or even your second. The weather and isolation was tough on everyone, but especially the young airman. Hell, I went to Minot kicking and screaming. But I made the best of it, and I had to put on a brave face for the airmen I supervised. I tried doing things like giving time off and having parties to make it a fun place to work, but at the end of the day, the mission came first. I also made some mistakes; it was my first time supervising two or more people, and I had five of them, all with different personalities. Richard made Minot a bearable place. His response to my message was refreshing and really made me proud to have served in the military:

```
Lorenzo,

Hmmmm, Good-looking fella, physically fit, impeccable
taste in nearly everything, no girlfriend, and lives
with his mother. No surprise here, my friend. I
have always been and always will be honored to have
served with you and to have had you as one of
my first supervisors. Thank goodness that DADT has
been repealed and individuals who choose a different
lifestyle can no longer be discriminated against in
the armed forces. Keep on keeping on, Lorenzo! It
sounds like you're doing great things!

Your pal,
Rich Van Dyke
```

Richard, I have a point of order: I did not live with my mother; she lived with me. I do appreciate the kind words, and it was truly my honor to have worked with and learned from you.

Okay, I sent out ten messages and received five responses. If I were doing research, I would be happy with a 50 percent response rate. I didn't expect to hear back from everyone. I'm still here, and nothing bad happened to me. It's hard to break the habit of living two lives.

I have such respect for the younger generation, gay and straight, for having open minds. As I open my mind to the possibility of truly living an openly gay lifestyle, I have to escape the fear of being rejected. As my friend Kenny might say, "All of this isn't for everyone," and that's okay. I do know that I cannot tell people how to react to my sexuality, but I can choose how I will react to or feel about them accepting or rejecting me. Now I have to live it!

Integrity First

I need to talk about the pink elephant in the room: integrity. In this book, I write about "integrity first" while also admitting that I concealed my sexuality throughout my military career. It's as if I'm talking out of both sides of my mouth. Having to hide my sexuality has been a source of great pain for me. Honestly, I feel like an onion, with many layers—and my sexuality is one layer. If you believe that one little layer on the inside means I don't have integrity, you have missed who I am and who I have been throughout my entire career.

I so admire the young folks of today. They live out loud and are very free about expressing their sexuality. Then again, the younger generation has grown up in a more tolerant world. When I grow up, I want to be more like them.

Taking the steps to write this book has helped free me from years of fear—fear of being rejected and fear of not fitting in. I know everyone will not agree with my choice to hide my sexuality in order to enter the Air Force and then continue to hide it so I could stay there. I was so sure that people knew my secret, or at least suspected it, throughout my career. I always thought they could tell just by looking at me.

The truth is, my situation kept me from forming lasting relationships with a lot of cool people. I'm sure people felt I was holding back at times. My closest friends knew all about me, but what's a shame is that I treated most of my family as I did my straight military friends until I turned thirty-five. The only two people who knew for sure that I was gay were my mother and my stepsister. It's true: your mother knows these things before you do.

Now back to the integrity issue. I'm not sure how to reconcile the notion of having integrity while covering up my sexuality. I'm not sorry that I joined the military; it was the best decision I ever made. The Air Force changed my life, opening me up to new cultures and, in a fashion, completing my transition from boy to man. A friend of mine, Dr. John Parkhurst, has said it was not the failed integrity of individuals, but rather that of the military that led to the institutional assumption that gays could not serve in the armed forces. As a result of this assumption, gay men and women who were fit to serve did so despite the fact that the institution deemed them unfit. The point is that people who questioned the integrity of closeted military personnel failed to see the injustice in DADT. These personnel were working for an institution whose integrity was compromised.

David has strong thoughts about core values like integrity. He felt that every day he put on the uniform, he was showing integrity, and it had nothing to do with being straight or gay. Conversely, he would say that what he did behind closed doors had nothing to do with his job or his workplace. Kenny, Ski, and David all find no issue with keeping your sexuality secret while serving in the military. In fact, both Kenny and David pointed out many instances of infidelity by our straight counterparts. We have a motto in the military: "What goes TDY (deployment) stays TDY." Where is the integrity in married people sleeping around with other married people on TDY? Ski also pointed out that gays and lesbians often covered for straight military personnel whose kids were sick, and many gays were selected for deployment or worked during the holidays because they did not have kids.

We have plenty of integrity—I agree with my friends. Thinking back, I guess the military agreed, as well. Repealing Don't Ask, Don't Tell eliminated any issues with integrity. Now that we have talked about the pink elephant in the room, I will let you draw your own conclusions about it.

Preparing the Military for the Repeal

It would be short-sighted not to address the notion that allowing gays to serve openly would be detrimental to military operations and that leadership would not be able to control the discriminatory actions of personnel. When I first heard these arguments, I imagined the same thing being said when African-Americans and women were integrated into the military. I was ashamed to hear such remarks, because they are poor excuses for blocking progress. After my twenty years of service, I can say that one thing holds true for all military personnel: we follow orders. If an order came down prohibiting any discrimination or hazing based on sexuality, military personnel would adhere to it.

The principle of following orders is an important one, because no leader wants to go to war with subordinates who cannot follow orders. We all know there are a few rotten apples in every barrel, so it's safe to assume that a few military personnel will not follow orders. This is not a new problem, and we know how to deal with it. If you are in a leadership position and feel you cannot follow orders, it's time for you to step aside, separate, or retire.

I remember reading a comment about how gays shouldn't be so "queeny," and while it pissed me off, I remembered back to the time when I felt that cross-dressers diminished the gay community because they lessened our ability to be viewed as "normal" by straight people. I realized I'd been hypocritical, because everyone has a right to live in his or her own way. It is also important to remember that those gays who will be serving openly still must adhere to military standards, and that fact isn't going to change.

I would like to commend Defense Secretary Robert Gates for having the courage to stand with President Obama on this issue. We have seen too much grandstanding and voting along political lines instead of doing what's right.

I will get off my soapbox now.

Well, the Defense Department certified on July 22, 2011, that it was ready to implement the repeal of Don't Ask, Don't Tell. The policy set in place training in all branches of the military to ensure standards for readiness, unit cohesion, recruitment, and retention. I cannot speak for the other branches of the service, but the Air Force has always conducted training on equal employment and sensitivity. There are guidelines for reporting violations and even more guidelines for conducting investigations.

I do have one concern about a long-standing rule that is rarely enforced. Recently I have seen several statements on the policy banning public displays of affection in the military. I'm assuming there will be a crackdown on everything, even holding hands and kissing. So how many times have you seen military personnel hug and kiss their loved ones when leaving for and returning from a deployment?

I'm reminded of the time I came out to my father. He accepted me and my lifestyle—as long as he did not have to see it or hear about it. Things changed as I helped him understand that this was not true acceptance. I hope this is not where we are heading with the military. Time will tell how policies change or are enforced in this new era.

Advice to Those Serving Openly

This is a very emotional time for most of us who served in silence. We feel that our sacrifices have paid off; current military personnel will not have to endure the same hardships we faced. This is a time to celebrate as you take your rightful place among heterosexuals in the military. You have the support of the president and the secretary of defense, and senior officials have provided guidance and implemented training for all military and civilian personnel. It will be your job to work out the kinks over the next couple of years.

Remember that water runs to the lowest level. Some people will revert to old habits and need a friendly reminder. It will not be your job to confront ignorance, but to identify it and let senior leadership handle it.

The bar is set high for you. We know that you will continue to serve with honor and perform at the highest level. You now serve on the backs of those who came before you. If you have integrity, strength, and love for your country, show it with your military bearing and outstanding professionalism. I have no facts to support this statement, but I believe gay people are naturally suited to shine and stand out from the pack. Do what we have always done, and history will write itself.

Conclusion

I made a wonderful discovery while writing this book. It was staring me right in the face, and I did not see it. My experiences and those of my friends reveal an important truth about the men and women in uniform: there has always been a place for gays and lesbians in the military, even if the institution itself wasn't ready for us. We weren't as clever as we thought at keeping our secret.

The truth is, our coworkers did not care about our sexuality. They cared that we did our jobs well. That's not to say they would not have turned us in with appropriate proof; military policy dictated it. But when you are in the trenches, you want to know that the person in there with you has your back—and I don't just mean on the battlefield. The daily grind of getting the peacetime mission completed also requires all hands on deck. When I was in the military, I had great respect for those who pulled their weight, and I believe my straight colleagues felt the same way.

I look forward to the day when everyone truly embraces the American notion of life, liberty, and the pursuit of happiness for all—something which, if you think about it, we "Americans" have not yet allowed. So far, it's

been more along the lines of, "You can have
these freedoms if you believe and think like I
do!" We have found too many reasons to block
people from the American dream.

I will admit that I have my own biases, but
I do not actively walk over other people's
rights when I do not agree with them. I embrace
those differences and see a world that is not
boring, because we are not drones, acting and
thinking the same. The end to Don't Ask, Don't
Tell and the passage of legislation allowing
gay marriage in several states tell me that we
are moving in the right direction—but there's
more work to do.

I'm not asking anyone to agree with me, but
I am asking for the right all Americans have
life, liberty, and the pursuit of happiness.

I thank David, Kenny, and Ski for sharing
their stories. After having lived such a
guarded life, it's not easy to open up. I hope
you the read see the patriotism and honor in
our service. A
common thread in
all our stories
is how we managed
our struggles in
silence. Although
there were times
when we could lean
on each other for
support, we were
not always in the
same location, so leaning on each other was
not easy. I make this point because I cannot
tell you how many times I had to listen to a
coworker's personal problems at work; I had to
be friend, counselor, confidant, coach, prayer

partner, and mediator. We all strive to keep personal issues out of the workplace, but that is not always possible. People feel comfortable telling me their personal problems. And I didn't mind helping my friends; I felt compelled to alleviate their pain. But while we were there for our straight colleagues, there was no one there for us. Had I shared my personal struggles with my coworkers, I risked the possibility of being outed or, even worse, turned in to the Office of Special Investigations. What kind of choice was that?

I remember many times when I was in pain over a personal issue but had to move through my workday as if nothing were wrong. But attentive people can always tell when there's something on your mind. When questioned by coworkers, I would lie or just say I hadn't slept well the night before. When I finally came out to one of my oldest military friends, Captain Shelia Grady, she said she felt bad about the countless times that she was able to lean on me when the reverse was not true. I'll admit I had the feeling that if I had confided in her, she would have kept my secret. However, it was a chance I could not take. There was too much at stake to be wrong.

My military friend Robert Spencer was actually mad at me for not having confided in him, and I believe there were other coworkers who would have been there for me, too. I'll never really know how events would have played out had I decided to confide in one of them. You know the saying—you tell one friend who tells two friends, and they tell two friends, and so on. Before you know it, everyone knows the secret.

While not every gay or lesbian serving in the military can say he or she was successful or had a stellar career, the majority of the ones I know have. David, Kenny, Ski, and I all enjoyed highly successful military careers despite the distractions of Don't Ask, Don't Tell and constantly having to look over our shoulders. I have no proof that DADT altered events in my life and who knows maybe things would have been

different—you can draw your own conclusions. What if we had been able to work without the distraction of having to hide and live in fear? Perhaps more important, what will this new generation be able to accomplish as openly gay and lesbian military personnel? I am excited to see what the future holds. I feel as if the restraints have been removed and my sisters and brothers are now free to excel in ways I only dreamed of. When I was in the military, I had to hold myself back at times so as not to draw attention to myself. This will no longer be the case for gay military personnel. With the repeal of DADT, I think the military will become stronger as it finally harnesses the full power of the gay and lesbian community.

When I went to bed on Monday, September 19, 2011, I realized it would be the last night of Don't Ask, Don't Tell. When I woke up the next morning, I felt like my struggles and those of so many others had finally paid off. As I got ready for work, however, the realization set in that the struggle was not over—that the men and women serving in the post-DADT military will need to be shining examples of the gay and lesbian community. They will be living in a fish bowl for the next year or two, with the whole world watching. Obviously, some people will be supportive, but others will be hoping and looking for reasons to say that the repeal of DADT was a mistake. I closed my eyes and offered up this prayer:

Lord, I give thanks for your many blessings and your sacrifice. On this day, I ask that you protect your gay and lesbian children. Provide a place of stillness and calm in troubled times. While we rejoice the repeal of Don't Ask, Don't Tell, allow us to be shining examples for the whole world to see. I pray that all military personnel follow orders and make this time of transition an orderly one. These things I ask in your name, Amen.

I have always lived by the motto that God will not place on you more than you can bear. I know that my sisters and brothers will be successful in this new era. If history teaches us anything, this integration will be as successful as the integration of blacks and women into the military.

There were two things that I never thought I would live to see: a black American president, and gays serving openly in the military. God is good, and I am so glad that I was here to witness these miracles.

About the Author

LORENZO L. MCFARLAND, DHA, MSW, PMP, is a veteran with twenty years of service. He retired at the rank of master sergeant, having served as an aerospace medicine technician and public health craftsman. Dr. McFarland was stationed at Zaragoza AB, Spain; Aviano AB, Italy; Minot AFB, North Dakota; and Brooks AFB, Texas. His awards include the Air Force Achievement Medal (three oak leaf clusters); the Air Force Commendation Medal (two oak leaf clusters); the NATO Medal; the Armed Forces Expeditionary Medal; the Meritorious Service Medal; and the Air Force Outstanding Unit (two silver leaf clusters).

Contributors

KENNETH N. BROOKS, MBA, is a twenty-one-year Air Force veteran serving as a weather technician. His assignments have included Aviano, Italy (two tours); Incirlik, Turkey (two tours); Sembach AB, Germany; Abilene, Texas; Fort Polk, Louisiana; and Omaha, Nebraska. His awards include the Air Force Achievement Medal (one oak leaf cluster); Air Force Commendation Medals; the Army Commendation Medal (three oak leaf clusters); and the Meritorious Service Medal (one oak leaf cluster).

BRIAN E. MARKOWSKI is an eight-year Air Force veteran serving as an aerospace ground equipment technician and telecommunications tech controller. His assignments have included Ramstein AB, Germany; Hurlburt Field, Florida; and Scott AFB, Illinois. His awards include Air Force Outstanding Unit Medals (two oak leaf clusters); the Air Force Good Conduct Medal (two oak leaf clusters); the Air Force Achievement Medal; the Combat Readiness Medal; and Air Force Airman of the Quarter (three times).

T. DAVID GILMER is a navy veteran with twenty years of service. His assignments have included Long Beach and San Diego, California; Louisville, Kentucky; Norfolk, Virginia; Naples, Italy; and Washington DC. His awards include a Combat Action Ribbon; the Joint Commendation Medal; the Joint Achievement Medal; the Navy Commendation Medal (silver oak leaf cluster); and the Navy Achievement Medal (four oak leaf clusters).